FLiCK nation presents
american popcorn
HOLLYWOOD AND THE WAR ON COMMON SENSE

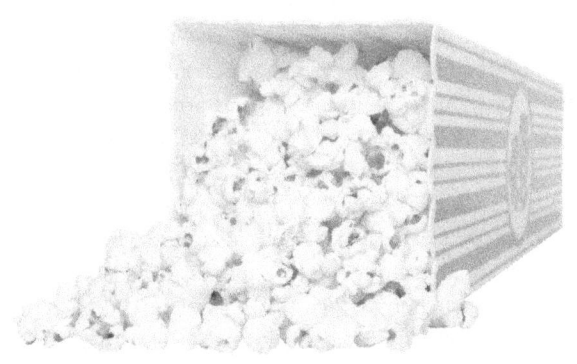

Dennis Willis

American Popcorn:
Hollywood and the War on Common Sense

Copyright © 2012 by Dennis Willis

ISBN-13: 978-1477543467
ISBN-10: 1477543465

PROMOTIONAL IMAGE CREDITS

Anchor Bay Entertainment, Columbia Pictures, Destination Films, Dimension Films, Disneynature, DreamWorks, Focus Features, Fox Atomic, Fox Searchlight, Hallmark Productions, HBO Films, IFC Films, Janus Films, Juno Films Inc., Koch-Lorber Films, Lionsgate Films, LucasFilm, Metro-Goldwyn-Mayer (MGM), Miramax Films, MTV Films, Nickelodeon Movies, New Line Cinema, Newmarket Films, Overture Films, Palm Pictures, Paramount Pictures, Paramount Vantage, Peace Arch Films, Picturehouse, Pixar, Saga Films Inc., The Samuel Goldwyn Company, Screen Gems, Sony Pictures Animation, Sony Pictures Classics, Sony Pictures Entertainment, Stage 6 Films, Strand Releasing, Summit Entertainment, The Weinstein Company, THINKFilm, Touchstone Pictures, TriStar Pictures, Triumph Films, Twentieth Century-Fox, United Artists, Universal Pictures, Walt Disney Pictures, Warner Bros., Warner Independent Pictures, Yari Film Group

Quentin Tarantino photos: Steven Underhill

FOR MY FATHER,

who I never thought even *liked* movies until the day he bought a
video store. He taught me how to look at art critically,
and that, sometimes, a good popcorn flick is all you need.

TaBLE OF conTEnTS

INTRODUCTION

Over the past 20 years, something interesting happened to the sports industry.

The overall conversation, which had never ventured past stats, averages and a general knowledge of standout players, slowly broadened until the casual fan was discussing management and coaching styles, following the draft process, and even rating teams based on how much their annual budget and salary caps are.

And because of this paradigm shift, Michael Lewis' 2003 book *Moneyball: The Art of Winning an Unfair Game* was able to flourish. This was a book about the Oakland A's, but not a dishy, dramatic tell-all. Nope, this was the exciting tale about how general manager Billy Beane used an analytical, sabermetric approach to assembling a competitive team, despite Oakland's small operational budget.

Even crazier? This book, chock full of statistics, inspired a hit 2011 movie with Brad Pitt and Jonah Hill!

The *business* of sports has so permeated the mainstream, that there are now entire networks dedicated to the intricacies. Fans not only understand it all, but are invested in what happens behind closed doors.

Not so in the entertainment industry.

On the one hand, you have "coming attractions" fluff like *Entertainment Tonight,* and on the other, you have TMZ, a website (and TV show) dedicated to following celebrities around and waiting for them to do or say something untoward.

But when it comes down to the nuts and bolts of salaries, global release patterns, movie budgets, and game-changing decisions, such as how converting the entire filmmaking and projection process to digital is not only affecting the future, but also how we gain access to the previous *hundred years of movies* ... well, the public at large isn't really having that conversation yet.

And yet, that's the most important part, the central argument, the eternal struggle in Hollywood:

Art vs. Commerce.

The creators want to make art. The suits want to make money. Somewhere in the middle lies the devil in the details. During the creation, production and selling of a film, endless compromises are made: the script must tell a good story, yet be accessible. The actors must be capable, but likable. The ending must be satisfying, yet not be a downer.

And no matter how powerful the director, chances are good that not even *they* can control what's revealed in the trailer, nor do they have much input when comments from focus groups convince upper management to re-edit their film to make it more likable, or easier to understand.

Art vs. Commerce.

When you consider all the compromises, it's amazing when any film can get it right. *That's* the conversation movie fans should be having, not talking about Tom Cruise jumping on couches and whatever crazy thing Charlie Sheen is up to.

A LITTLE HISTORY

Before I worked with Steve Wagner on the *Flick Nation* radio show, we had a TV show called *Reel Life*, which ran for five years during the 90s. We began each week with about five minutes of industry commentary and discussion about projects and trends that would ultimately shape what we see on the big screen.

Even though we owned the show, by the time we reached an ABC affiliate, it was re-dubbed *FilmTrip* and management wanted to turn it into *Entertainment Tonight*: more fluff, more rumors, more movie stars - because, you know, that's what people want to see. That, and more arguing during the review segments. And maybe a hand puppet of Marlon Brando. I'm not even kidding about that.

Our idea of art vs. their idea of commerce.

Needless to say, our show was ultimately canceled, but I continued a weekly feature on KGO Radio, which kept me seeing and reviewing films every week.

My day job was running Video Plus, my family's video store since 1986. It wasn't the most successful store in town but we did okay, and it was always fun talking to people about movies. People knew I was a critic and they were willing to share their opinions. I loved that part.

Regarding critical analysis, when the decade began, there was just Siskel and Ebert. But by the close of the 90s, the internet had exploded, leveling the playing field for just about anyone with a computer. It seemed the only thing more available than porn was film critics.

In 1999, I launched *Soundwaves Cinema,* a movie-oriented website that provided reviews and commentary. Like the store, it was a modest hangout for all involved, including the handful of talented writers willing to accept free movies as their payment.

About that time, Pacifica Tribune publisher Chris Hunter asked me to write a weekly column that I would later post online. When I told him I didn't necessarily want to just review movies, he grew even more interested. The more "inside baseball" I got, the more he encouraged me.

I covered movies, TV, release patterns, deals and spoke out about whatever else was on my mind that week.

Most times, I looked no further than my own desk. The politics of the video industry were fascinating at the time: the VHS format had just begun its death spasm, and DVD was gathering steam. Some movies were priced at over a hundred bucks, while the same movie on DVD was under $20. The whole industry was getting shakier by the minute.

A DECADE AND CHANGE

In the past decade, just about everything changed. Major movie stars such as Tom Hanks and Jim Carrey lost their mojo when studios shifted their priorities to focus on a global strategy in which high-concept flicks like *Pirates of the Caribbean* and *Transformers* could play around the world with very little lost in translation.

Video stores died - our own store closed in 2007 - and the entire industry gave way to Redbox vending machines, downloads, both legal and illegal, and streaming. In 2012, more money will be generated from "internet" rentals and sales than physical discs.

The *Blair Witch Project* (1999) introduced the mainstream to the "found footage" cinema vérité style, but Hollywood studios couldn't figure out a way to capitalize on it until *Paranormal Activity* (2008). Since then, we've gotten "found footage" movies about haunted houses and exorcisms (*The Last Exorcism, The Devil Inside*), teen parties (*Project X*) and superheroes (*Chronicle*), all on the cheap.

Once again, studios trotted out the old 3D format, and this time it stuck, for two reasons. It was embraced by visionary filmmakers such as James Cameron and Martin Scorsese, but mainly because studios realized they could charge a premium ticket price, thereby inflating their profits, even as audiences continued to erode.

ABOUT THAT GALAXY FAR, FAR AWAY...

Apparently, the countdown to the release of *Star Wars, Episode I: The Phantom Menace* (1999) was kind of a big deal. I'd forgotten exactly how much weight was placed on that film, but was surprised to find my coverage captured the universally-recognized phenomenon among old-school *Star Wars* fans: that dreaded moment when you realize not only are they *just movies*, but not all of them are classics.

When *Star Wars* (1977) was released, it rocked my 10-year-old world. I was first in line for the 1997 Special Editions, and ready for the prequels. At one point, I even boldly proclaimed they would change film as we know it. The jury is still out on that one, but they certainly illuminated many of creator George Lucas' limitations as a writer and director.

I think the core *Star Wars* fans would have accepted three lackluster prequels just fine. But Lucas kept messing with the original trilogy: first a few special FX touch-ups, then a few new scenes, and finally, changing the character-building blocks fans had come to love over twenty-plus years.

Lucas began to complain about his own fans, which is not exactly the best way to engender a faithful following. There was even a documentary called *The People vs. George Lucas.*

THE WAR ON COMMON SENSE

It seems that every other day, there is a new war being fought: a war on drugs, on Christmas, on women, on culture. But even though Hollywood is America's greatest export to the world, and the most consistent revenue generator in these tough economic times, nobody ever calls the studios on their bullshit?

When was the last time you saw an Occupy Hollywood movement about the cynical, soulless machines that sell us remakes, sequels and reboots, shows us all the good parts in the trailers and then charges an extra fee for "XD" or barely noticeable, fuzzy 3D?

Everyone loves movies, and yet we have settled into an abusive relationship with the powers that be. They serve us the same watered-down focus group-approved pap and treat us like sheep, we respond by giving them *billions*!

And believe me, *I love movies*!

This book is a collection of reviews and columns spanning 13 years, handpicked by theme. But whether talking about TV, *Star Wars* or Hollywood development, I realized my weekly blatherings kept returning to the primal theme of art vs. commerce.

And yet, re-reading these articles only make me realize that the more things change, the more they stay exactly the same.

With the exception of cleaning up some grammar, the essays and columns have not been altered. My thoughts, however clever or misinformed, were my opinions at the time. In a few cases, I provide a historical or personal postscript, to either rethink my position or claim a little victory at brilliant foreshadowing.

But in the end, we all know what opinions are like.

Art will always be about the creative process, the ego, the big picture and the impact on humanity. Commerce will take the art, brand it, package it, and through focus groups, grind down the edges to make it more sellable.

Art needs commerce. Commerce needs art. But rarely, if ever, are they good for each other.

All an audience wants is to be entertained. Like sports, all those boring statistics and budgets mean nothing if the game is thrilling, a shared experience to remember forever.

At the end of the day, ain't that the point?

1 MIDDLE-AGE
CRAZY
...OR HOW SOME PEOPLE JUST CAN'T HELP THEMSELVES.

Every successful career in Hollywood is, more or less, exactly the same. Actors and filmmakers start out happy to have a job and eager to leave a mark. After years of hard work and a burst of initial success, they find themselves in the enviable position to seek out interesting projects that allow them to develop their original voices, but not *too* original, for they must also appeal to the mainstream.

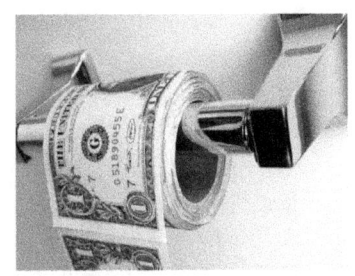

Most actors and filmmakers fortunate enough to eventually earn the mantle of "legend" (or at least, "veteran") do so after they find a happy medium between art and commerce.

I'm interested in what happens in the middle.

At some point, armed with a rare combination of career momentum and hubris, the artist decides to express themselves. And let me tell you, that is usually the moment the training wheels come off. Some risks pay off, but others stumble into the abyss more spectacularly than others. Harrison Ford and John Travolta, I'm looking at you.

When that rare combination of prestige and ego kicks in, you never know what you're going to get. In the classic *Chinatown* (1974), John Huston said the immortal line "Politicians, ugly buildings, and whores all get respectable if they last long enough."

The same goes for actors and directors.

Harrison Bored: When Harry Met Salary

February 2, 2000

In the 1988 movie *Scrooged*, Bill Murray referred to John Houseman as "America's favorite old fart." In the decade or so since, I'd say that torch has successfully been passed to the man most associated with box office hits than any other this generation: Harrison Ford.

Before you call me blasphemous for dissing Indiana Jones, think about it. After *The Fugitive*, he began earning $20 million salaries and seemed to fall asleep at the wheel. Think I'm wrong?

Let's examine the evidence:

He was at least 15 years too old to play Jack Ryan. *The Devil's Own* ran over-budget and made back less than half its cost. Even worse, what was it? A drama? A political thriller? Not even the movie knew.

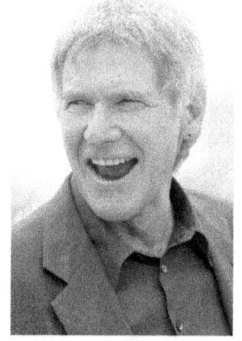

In *Six Days Seven Nights*, he might have been playing Indy's drunken older brother. Most embarrassing was when (with shirt open) he single-handedly whupped a handful of strapping young weapon-toting banditos. Even Steven Seagal's been more believable lately. He mumbled and twitched through *Sabrina*, and put audiences to sleep in *Random Hearts*.

His only real hit since then, *Air Force One*, sported one of those catchy one-sentence pitches: Harrison Ford is the butt-kicking president.

Recently, he defended his bloated salary as "the going rate."

But the reason I'm choosing now to pick on Harry is because if the rumors are true, he's considering a role in director Steven Soderbergh's next film, *Traffic*, an ambitious ensemble piece in which he would forgo his usual salary and play a supporting role, alongside Catherine Zeta-Jones and others. Why is this reason to break out the bubbly?

To paraphrase Han Solo, the reasons could fill a space cruiser. First off, take a look at Nick Nolte, Robin Williams, and Tom Cruise. After years of playing lead roles in big Hollywood films, all three recently took gritty character turns, resulting in the best reviews of their careers.

Cruise will most likely land a Best Supporting Actor Oscar nomination for *Magnolia*; Williams won the same category for *Good Will Hunting* two years ago. Even Sylvester Stallone's turn in *Cop Land* erased a decade's worth of Rambo jokes. I tell you, it works.

This would give Ford the opportunity to cut loose and play one of those scrappy bastards he played so well in movies like *The Mosquito Coast* or *Presumed Innocent*.

Also, isn't it about time Ford changed his shtick a little? The man is pushing sixty and starting to look a little silly beating up bad guys or playing exaggerated boy scouts. If I see that half-smile (irony) or those twitchy fingers (concern) one more time, I'm gonna go postal.

Ford was nominated for an Academy Award for *Witness* in 1986, and for a while, he seemed to be seeking out roles that would require him to act. He played the impossible Allie Fox to perfection in Peter Weir's *The Mosquito Coast*, and followed that with Roman Polanski's *Frantic* in 1988. Both went largely forgotten, save for that line in the Barenaked Ladies song. "Like Harrison Ford, I'm getting frantic..." Well, at least *somebody* saw it.

But after the third Indiana Jones movie and a lateral move into the Jack Ryan series when (the better cast) Alec Baldwin opted out, Ford became complacent. The irony is that while *The Fugitive* was nominated for Best Picture in 1993, many felt Ford should have scored a nod for his nearly dialogue-free Richard Kimble, a breakthrough in controlled and intelligent intensity.

What happened beyond that remains a mystery, but this much is true: Harrison Ford in a Steven Soderbergh ensemble would be ten times hipper than that earring he's been sported, or all his pathetic appearances on *The Tonight Show*. It would reinvent our greatest movie star as a Sean Connery-level actor ready to enter the next phase of his career.

Soderbergh, who directed *Out Of Sight*, my favorite film of 1998, has a great reputation with actors. Hell, he single-handedly rescued George Clooney from *Batman and Robin* and pointed him toward good movies. And think about this: Clooney's last two films have out-grossed Ford's by $30 million.

Harrison Ford doesn't need another check for "the going rate." He needs to get angry, get fat, grow a beard, play a bad guy, work with other actors, do *something*.

POSTSCRIPT:

Ford never took the role in *Traffic*, which went to Michael Douglas instead. He also passed on the role in Soderbergh's *Syriana* that won George Clooney his first Academy Award. But he thought *Firewall* was a good idea?

When it comes to picking on Ford, turns out I was ahead of my time. There are websites and Facebook groups devoted to images of Harrison Ford simply pointing at people from his movies.

He had a couple of moderate hits, but his biggest non-Indiana Jones role was that of a villain in *What Lies Beneath*. His roles in *K-19: The Widowmaker* (2002), *Hollywood Homicide* (2003), *Firewall* (2006), and *Extraordinary Measures* (2010) were all met with yawns at the box office.

Travolta Spaces Out
May 17, 2000

See, the thing is, I like John Travolta. I think he's a talented actor, who, when directed by a Quentin Tarantino or a John Woo, can find nuances in any given performance, scene, or moment. He's truly one of our great movie stars. He can sing, he can dance, and he can be frightening or endearing.

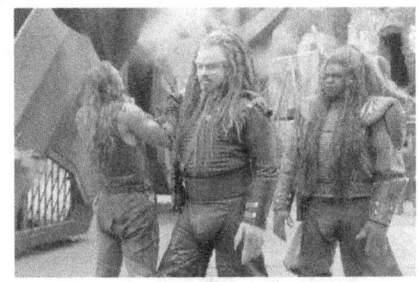

But there are reasons why *Battlefield Earth* was never made into a film before, not the least of which is that after predators, terminators and aliens to chew on, how scary - *really* - can the Psychlos possibly be?

They're big and goofy looking, they walk funny, and call each other things like "crap head" with all of the aplomb of someone from the mid-1950's, much less the year 3000.

Travolta apparently made getting this book to the big screen his prime directive and, well, he certainly accomplished it. I just hope next time, he chooses something a little more accessible, like *Scientology For Dummies*.

It's not just that Travolta is completely over the top as the evil Terl (pronounce TEH-ruhl), the whole movie is preposterous. Get this: the evil Psychlos have ruled Earth for a thousand years, and refer to us as "man animals." They keep us in cages, and at their mercy.

Oh, but just wait.

Terl develops a plan to get off this miserable planet, but it will require silly humans to mine gold for him. Enter Jonnie "Goodboy" Tyler (I'm not kidding), who is played with zeal by Barry Pepper, doing his best *Braveheart* impersonation. Before you can say plot contrivance, he is taught the history, language and secrets of the Psychlos in no time flat.

Terl brings Jonnie and his rag-tag group of buddies to the remote drilling area in Denver, Colorado -- and just LEAVES! He tells them he will be back in 14 days, which is just enough time for our heroes to fly to Washington D.C., learn everything about human

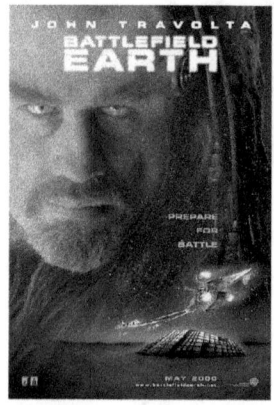

history, plan a revolt, get to Texas, and learn to fly Harrier jets, still perfectly preserved after almost 1000 years!

I guess nobody was thinking the audience would question the effectiveness of jets, bullets, fuel, tracking systems and heat seeking missiles after a millennium. This movie teaches us that in a thousand years, they'll be good as new.

Battlefield Earth was bad in ways I forgot a movie could be. It got everything wrong. *Everything.* Even the 9-foot Psychlos couldn't walk without looking like wobbly actors on stilts. Travolta's Terl sports big fake flappy hands that bend back whenever he tries to pick something up.

Director Roger Christian might have won an Academy Award (for set decoration on George Lucas's original Star Wars) but seems powerless to "direct" anything. Whenever he runs into trouble with a scene (almost all of them), he breaks a lot of glass and frames the action in dutch-angle slow motion.

I kid you not; at least a third of the action in *Battlefield Earth* happens in slow motion. If they had just played the damn thing at regular speed, it could have been over in 75 minutes.

In every major career, there's always at least one of these: a vanity project that gets produced only because a major star throws his or her weight, passion, and resources into it - and more times than not, it's a tactical error, and a stinkeroo to boot.

Bruce Willis had his *Hudson Hawk*. Dustin Hoffman and Warren Beatty had their *Ishtar* (even though Warren's *Town and Country* lost more money). And Kevin Costner had his, well, where do you want me to start?

Like I said before, I think Travolta is very talented. But we all know what the road to hell is paved with, even if Scientologists don't believe in hell. Whoever pays full price to endure 117 minutes of this film will believe. Oh, yes. They will.

Battlefield Earth is thus far, the bottom scraper of 2000, a career low for Travolta, and one of the worst films of the past decade. Not even Alan Smithee would want his name on this.

POSTSCRIPT:

Battlefield Earth swept the 2000 Golden Raspberry Awards and received seven Razzies, including Worst Movie of the Year, Worst Actor (Travolta), Worst Supporting Actor (Pepper), Worst Supporting Actress (Preston), Worst Director (Christian), Worst Screenplay (Mandell and Shapiro), and Worst Screen Couple (Travolta and "anyone sharing the screen with him").

In 2010, the film received an award for "Worst Picture of the Decade," bringing its total number of Razzie Awards to nine and consequently setting a record for the most Razzies won by a single film. That record was surpassed in 2012 when *Jack and Jill* won ten awards.

Steven Seagal's Disappearing Act

April 5, 2000

Move over, Monica Lewinsky. Steven Seagal's back in town.

If all goes according to plan, Warner Bros. will distribute *Exit Wounds*, a return to form for the beefy action movie star, with Joel Silver producing and Andrzej Bartkowiak *Romeo Must Die* directing.

Silver's official statement: "People are interested in these kinds

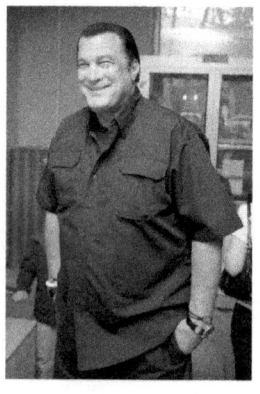

of films again, the hard-edged action film geared toward a young male audience. Research has told us that the audience is still there for Steven. *The Matrix* raised the bar, and so the challenge is to reinvent the genre, so that it feels cool, like *Romeo Must Die* feels cool."

The deal clincher was the contractual agreement that Seagal shed a little weight - okay, *a lot* of weight - and return to the trim fighting form he had in 1988's *Above The Law*. I think we can all agree that ol' Steven's looked liked he's lifted more turkey legs than weights in the past few years.

Don't get me wrong. I'm no svelte Tom Cruise myself. But when I can hold up the video box for *The Patriot*, and think to myself that I'm in better shape than Seagal, something's wrong.

To recap, Seagal's career took off like a bullet with *Above The Law*, and pretty much stayed on course with no-brainers like *Hard To Kill*, *Out For Justice*, and *Marked For Death*. But it was 1992's *Under Siege* (directed by *The Fugitive's* Andrew Davis and co-starring Tommy Lee Jones) that made a whopping $80 million. That was the beginning of the end.

Next, Warner gave Seagal $40 million to direct (!) an environmentally-themed action flick called *On Deadly Ground* that somehow attracted such co-stars as Michael Caine, Joan Chen and Billy Bob Thornton.

But the movie only made half of what *Under Siege* made, so of course, we knew what Seagal's next move would be. You guessed it: *Under Siege 2*, which ran over budget and made even less money. Have you ever seen the *Die Hard* on a train flick? Jeez, it was like a train wreck, itself, getting worse and worse as the running time progressed.

Not only that, but his acting was getting more and more lazy - a sure sign that the ego was starting to run amok.

In 1996, he played a supporting part in *Executive Decision*, and even allowed himself to die onscreen. In 1997, he appeared as himself in Billy Crystal's Hollywood satire *My Giant*, and allowed a kid to tell him he sucks. He was the best thing about either film, and offered hope that maybe he could poke a little fun at himself.

But then the bad action flicks continued: In *Fire Down Below*, he played an environmentally savvy man of action who came to a small town to settle down, only to find trouble.

In *The Patriot*, he played exactly the same role. But in *The Glimmer Man*, he was described as a man so fast that one could only catch a glimmer of him when he moved.

What, to the fridge?

By that time, Seagal was so out of shape that he appeared in almost every shot wearing black, at night, or half-hidden by bad lighting. His martial arts became slow motion trick photography, and his core audience knew it. His last three films released theatrically each made less than $20 million, while costing double.

The Patriot was shot for $43 million through independent financing and rejected by every major studio. The only money came from HBO, who shelled out $3 million to premiere it, and whatever Touchstone Home Video paid to dump it into the video market.

Inexplicably, his core audience didn't care.

They rented the hell out of *The Patriot*, even when they knew it was going to blow chunks.

That makes Steven Seagal sort of like everyone's favorite uncle. Everybody likes the guy, but only enough to look forward to visiting every other holiday. The fact is, in terms of Hollywood longevity, there are only so many roles out there written for retired, flabby eco-minded heroes. And Seagal's cornered that market.

Here's my two cents: Steven Seagal is making a smart move by dropping weight and aligning himself with a hip director. He should also alternate between comedy and dramas more, and allow himself the small, juicy supporting role here and there.

It also wouldn't be a bad thing to feature him as the villain.

He broods a lot and doesn't exactly have the warmest presence going. Oh, and Steven: Let somebody kick *your* butt once in a while. Goes a long way toward endearing yourself to an audience.

He should also be looking for a hip, scrappy little project to get involved with. Let's not forget John Travolta's name made people chuckle before he made *Pulp Fiction*.

Thus far, the action bruiser has dropped about 30 pounds and has three more months of training to go. So to the 48-year old Seagal, I say you go, boy.

Shake up that image a bit. You can join the ranks of Travolta, Sylvester Stallone and Sean Connery, who saw the writing on the wall and changed their career trajectory for the better.

Or you can follow the examples of Treat Williams, Jean Claude Van Damme and Christopher Lambert, who, well, didn't.

Costner: For Love Of The Fame

May 3, 2000

We've all seen it happen. An A-list actor lets his or her ego decide that it's not enough to be rich and successful. Nope, they wake up one day deciding to expand their reach by, say, writing a book of poems ... or deciding they want to write, direct or God forbid, sing on their own soundtrack.

These unfortunate acts of career self-mutilation must be stopped before they ruin all the hard work their publicists and agents have gone through. Celebrity suicide is hard to spot when said celebrity has a Best Director win under his belt for his first film.

But the truth must be faced. Kevin Costner must be stopped.

It was bad enough when *Dances With Wolves* (1990) stole the

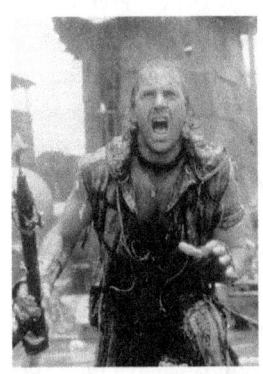

Best Picture and Director Oscars from Martin Scorsese's *GoodFellas*. But witness *Robin Hood: Prince Of Thieves* (1991) with his early 90's haircut and horrendous attempt at a British accent.

Sure, there was some solid post-Oscar character work: Clint Eastwood's *A Perfect World* (1993), the Vietnam-era coming-of-age drama *The War* (1994), and of course, Oliver Stone's *J.F.K.* (1991). But for every director who sits on Costner, there are five others who allow him to be Kevin Costner: Movie Star.

At this time, it's important to point out that in the life of every self-destructing celebrity is a dysfunctional counterpart who enables them. For Kevin Costner, that person is director Kevin Reynolds, who helmed Costner's first starring role in *Fandango* (1985). It was Reynolds who let Costner use that damned accent in *Robin Hood,* and he who allowed *Waterworld* (1995) to balloon to a then-unheard-of $175 million budget. Costner apparently had Reynolds fired during *Waterworld's* post-production, and oversaw the editing of the film, himself.

Some relationships are just bad news. But after all the drama, the two Kevins have just announced they are making another film together. Well, break out the wine and cut the cheese! And what project was so big, so tempting, that Costner and Reynolds agreed to hold hands and once again jump into the fray?

Okracoke.

Everybody say it together, because unless one of these knuckleheads grows some common sense, it's going to make a lot of headlines in the coming months.

The Legend of Okracoke is the story of a disgraced British (STRIKE ONE) Naval officer who becomes obsessed (STRIKE TWO) with finding and killing Blackbeard the pirate (STRIKE THREE).

First of all, pirate flicks don't make money. Period. Even Steven Spielberg's *Hook*, which had Robin Williams as Peter Pan barely made a profit. Then, there was Robert Altman's *Pirates*, *The Pirate Movie* and The *Pirates Of Penzance*. Oh, you forgot them already?

But the one that had all of Hollywood shivering its timbers was *Cutthroat Island*, the $100 million Geena Davis opus that lost so much money, it buried its studio, Carolco.

And let's face it; the Kevins don't exactly cut corners. When Kevin Costner does ANYTHING other than simply act in a film, you know at least one of the following things will happen:

A. The movie will be at least three hours long.

B. It will be filled with embarrassing vanity shots and/or slow motion horseback riding.

C. He may even sing the closing theme.

I realize that most people never made it to the end of *The Postman*, but Kev does warble over the final, agonizing moments of that one.

Most importantly, Costner flicks don't make that much money anymore. Even his last two sure shots - the baseball flick *For Love Of The Game* and weepie *Message In A Bottle* underperformed.

So, if the studio behind this atrocity doesn't pull the plug and this $100+ million pirate flick with an accent-spouting Costner gets made, it's up to us to do the right thing - THE RESPONSIBLE THING - and mercy kill this thing where it lands.

No matter what device they try to use to fool us, be it a snazzy trailer or Bryan Adams music video, we cannot be fooled. Kevin Costner needs an intervention. He must be stopped.

Perhaps if we act now, his career can still be saved. I mean, there's always direct-to-video work and CBS' action block on Saturday nights. Or that live musical stage version of *My Cuba* he plans to star in.

Come to think of it, maybe it's too late.

POSTSCRIPT:
This was clearly written before Disney's *Pirates of the Caribbean* became a billion dollar franchise. And thankfully, *The Legend of Okracoke* never saw the light of day.

But I have to say that since he's retreated to character roles, Costner has won me over again. He was the best thing about *The Company Men* (2011), as well as *Open Range* (2003, which he directed) and *The Upside of Anger* (2005).

Costner did eventually re-team with Reynolds for the 2012 miniseries *Hatfields & McCoys*, which nabbed massive ratings for History Channel, even if it ran six hours!

Shyamalan: The Last Bender

June 30, 2010

In 2002, Newsweek Magazine famously announced that auteur M. Night Shyamalan was "the next Spielberg." Based on the strength of *The Sixth Sense*, which made half a billion dollars, scared up six Oscar nominations and ushered in a new appreciation for twist endings ... sure, okay.

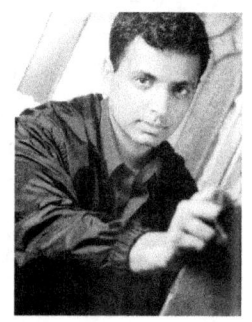

After *Unbreakable* (2000) and *Signs* (2002), Night began a merciless slide into mediocrity and unintentional self-parody. After the awful eco-thriller *The Happening* (2008), the next Spielberg announced he would make a big splashy CGI-laden based on the beloved animated series *Avatar: The Last Airbender*, a property that already had a built-in audience. After years of diminishing creative and financial results, it was pretty much his only move.

The result: *The Last Airbender* is the worst movie of the year.

I suppose the term "worst" is relative. *Jonah Hex* was a bigger disaster. But *Jonah Hex* wasn't directed by a guy once nominated for a Best Director Oscar. Grading on a curve is a bitch.

I knew nothing about the story going in and I'm not sure I understand it any better having seen the film. I guess there are four world nations based on the elements – air, water, earth and fire.

As we begin, Fire Nation wants to rule everything, a plan interrupted by the mysterious appearance of Aang (Noah Ringer), a kid with a tattooed face who may or may not be the long-missing Avatar, the human embodiment of perfection and grace, like Jesus or the Dali Lama.

It is said the Avatar can bend all four elements but Aang can only control the air. Turns out a hundred years ago, he bolted from training when he learned about the "chosen one's" solitary and celibate lifestyle. So now it's a hundred years later and he's still 12 and only partially trained. Karate Kid, meet Anakin Skywalker.

There is also a wronged Fire Nation prince (Dev Patel), a 14-year girl waterbender (Nicole Peltz) and a big flying thing that looks like a cross between the dog creature in *The Neverending Story* and an otter. The movie is presented in 3D but don't be fooled: this is the same muddy after-the-fact slapdash conversion used on *Clash of the Titans* and makes everything look fuzzy.

The plot of "Book One" is about learning about Aang learning how to control water but let's face it, there aren't going to be any sequels. This sucker cost $280 million to make and market and without any emo vampires or shirtless werewolves, there is no way this movie is making that back.

I have no problem with the far-out concept. I've thrown my support behind orcs, wizards, Jedis and hot tub time machines all in the name of a good time. But this film is an unwatchable disaster. It lumps ahead from one half-baked sequence to the next, connecting everything that happens off-screen by way of ham-fisted narration, *telling* us everything and showing us nothing.

When a character shows up announcing they'd found a rare scroll with the keys to accomplishing an impossible task, why didn't we see them find the scroll? When Aang is called out for looking preoccupied he confesses that he'd been summoned by some sort of talking dragon demon. Yep, that happens off-screen too.

And when Aang finally summons up his water mojo, the climax ends up being a scene right out of James Cameron's *The Abyss* (the director's cut).

And for a kid who's supposed to be some kind of reincarnated second coming, he sure manages to get kidnapped a lot. At one point, he escapes by using his powers to blow people against walls while he flies away. There are a half dozen other times that same trick might have come in handy. I could go on forever.

The young actors never once come close to playing actual characters, much less ones from a specific fantasy world. It's clear that the band of youngsters were cast based on how attractive they were and not on their raw thespian abilities. They all talk with the urgency of going to the mall when not fretting, pouting, snarling, wincing, flirting, etc.

Poor Dev Patel might have been the heart of Best Picture winner *Slumdog Millionaire* (2008) but spends the bulk of this film glowering like a wet kitten.

I'd be tempted to spread around the generous blame had the first credit at the end of the flick not been "WRITTEN, PRODUCED AND DIRECTED BY M. NIGHT SHYAMALAN." Strip away all the whiz-bangy CGI stuff and attractive landscape that he had nothing to do with and we're left with a series of half-scenes that amount to one big montage.

The dialogue either describes things we can see or recounts things that have already happened. This is a guy who once constructed an entire film around the tricky idea that a kid can see dead people with precise scene-by-scene storytelling trickery.

What the hell happened to him?

Considering the pedigree of the award-winning source material, the vast amounts of production money and the generously-honored auteur steering this mess, *The Last Airbender* is probably the worst movie ever made by a former Oscar nominee.

It's not *Battlefield Earth* bad, but its close.

It's more like *Congo* bad.

Bringing Out The Dead: Scorsese Flatlines

October 27, 1999

In 1995, I was one of the few to not fall in line praising *Casino*, Martin Scorsese's thematic follow-up to *GoodFellas*.

In my opinion, *Casino* was a bloated retread without the spark or energy of the original. Scorsese even used Rolling Stones' "Gimme Shelter" to punctuate a similar moment as he did in *GoodFellas*.

I bring this up because in comparison to *Bringing Out The Dead*, *Casino* was an absolute work of concentration. On paper, his sprawling saga about a burned out paramedic in New York seems like an inspired return to the mean streets of the Big Apple. After all, he's directing from a Paul Schrader (*Taxi Driver*) script and has Nicolas Cage driving the ambulance.

What could possibly go wrong? Just about everything.

Bringing Out The Dead covers 56-hours in the life of Frank Pierce (Cage), a fast-working doc clinging to sanity after the ghosts of lost patients begin speaking to him. But now, he's hearing voices of victims before they die and seeing the face of Rose (Cynthia Roman), a patient he failed to save several 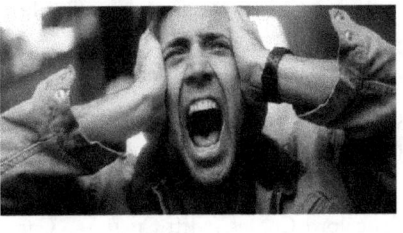 months earlier. His rotating partners barely notice, as they all seem to balance a certain mania while saving lives in the big city.

The callous insensitivity of the men and women who save lives is such a running joke, there could have been a laugh track.

Look, there's Noel (Marc Anthony), the crazed homeless guy who shows up in the ER more than some of the doctors, and he's doing something wacky. Audience laughs.

There's Tom Sizemore beating up on patients. Audience laughs.

There's Patricia Arquette suddenly freaking out in an elevator. Audience laughs.

Whoops. That's where Scorsese underestimates his audience. By crafting a sort of manic ER, he's programming us to laugh at the shenanigans, but then expects us to take Cage's torment seriously. And it's too bad.

Nicolas Cage is more introverted and focused then he's been since *Leaving Las Vegas*. It was a welcome experience to see him acting again, as opposed to doing his action film thing.

Rhames chews as much scenery as possible, and as the aggressive Christian Marcus, delivers the best line in the film. The performances are all solid. Problem is that while the actors know this is an actor's film, the director does not.

If so, Scorsese would have set his generally-observant camera down and watched the nuances of his actors explode off the screen. But instead of seeing an awkward Cage and Arquette sharing a long ambulance ride, we get a Natalie Merchant pop song telling us that these are the days...

Scorsese uses so many damned songs on the soundtrack; it was obvious he looked no further than his own CD collection for inspiration.

Individual scenes are powerful: the rescue of compassionate drug lord Coates (Cliff Curtis) ... Cage's breakdown in said dealer's pleasure pad, The Oasis ... the ultimate solution to a lingering patient who's body refuses to die even after 14 jump starts. But these scenes, while being great moments, are considerably less than the sum of their parts.

Bringing Out The Dead crumbles under its own inconsistencies. Cage's voice-over is irritatingly omnipresent for the first third and then gone. John Goodman shows up for the first quarter and disappears, to be replaced by Rhames and then Sizemore.

Maybe the rotating-door approach was meant to further support the idea that Frank's life has nothing to ground him from the images that haunt him, but it renders the film episodic.

In the end, *Bringing Out The Dead* feels like an overlong pilot for a TV series about unpredictable, but funny, guys who juggle God complexes with spasms of guilt. I knew that all would be okay in the end, that our heroes would live to fight another day.

And that's something I never felt while watching *Casino*.

Joe Pesci, all is forgiven.

POSTSCRIPT:

There are times I love being wrong, and in the case of Scorsese, I'm elated. The late-90s weren't kind to Marty, and my deepest fears were that his best years were in the rear view. And while he'll likely never deliver another *Mean Streets* (1973) *Taxi Driver* (1976), *Raging Bull* (1980), or *GoodFellas* (1990) again, the new century has seen the legendary auteur enter his most prolific and acclaimed period.

He finally won his Oscar for *The Departed* (2006), a vicious all-star crime epic, and has continued to churn out acclaimed crowd-pleasers such as *Gangs of New York* (2002), *The Aviator* (2004), *Shutter Island* (2010), and *Hugo* (2011).

But Scorsese's greatest evolution has been into an acclaimed documentarian with all the urgency of his masterful fictional work. His musical docs *No Direction Home: Bob Dylan* (2005), *A Letter to Ella* (2010), *George Harrison: Living in the Material World* (2011) and the theatrical Rolling Stones concert doc *Shine a Light* (2008) are all worth checking out.

Fear and Loathing in Puerto Rico

October 28, 2011

In 1998, Johnny Depp starred in the drug-fueled opus *Fear and Loathing in Las Vegas*, based on the novel by legendary gonzo journalist Hunter S. Thompson.

Depp and Thompson would become good friends, and while working on *Loathing*, Depp unearthed a box containing an unfinished manuscript for a book called *The Rum Diary*.

It was Thompson's first attempt at writing the Great American Novel, based on his coming-of-age working for a small newspaper in Puerto Rico in 1959. The book was eventually finished, a fitting finale to the tale's 40-year journey and a fitting coda to Thompson's incendiary oeuvre. *The Rum Diary* is filled with possibility, with the desire to write stories and change the world.

It has an optimistic streak throughout, even while evil capitalists solidify the young writer's worldview to fight corruption and "get the bastards." This background is worth noting to understand where the film version of *The Rum Diary* fails. It's the story of a young artist finding his voice, wooed by a beautiful woman, and deciding that standing up to corruption is the only worthy position to take.

Reading Thompson's work, one gets the impression that taking the bastards down wasn't just a hobby, it was his prime directive. He was a literary Superman fighting for truth, justice and the American way. There are only glimpses of that character here.

Depp plays a hard-partying American freelance journalist named Paul Kemp who takes a job at the Puerto Rican rag The San Juan Star. But despite what he's called in the movie, everyone knows he's playing a young Thompson, a point made all the more apparent when you realize he's playing the same character he played in *Fear and Loathing*, albeit with less hair and more drugs.

Kemp is wooed by smooth-taking filthy-rich businessman Sanderson, (Eckhart), who wants him to write flattering things about a corrupt hotel development deal that's about to go down on a remote island. Sanderson's reach becomes apparent when he comes

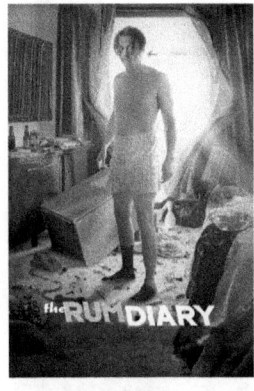 to Kemp's rescue in a politically-impossible situation, but it's still not enough to convince the writer that greed is good.

Besides, Kemp is taken with Chenault, Sanderson's sultry but vacant fiancée (Heard), who first appears out of nowhere taking a midnight swim. There are comedic asides with his two pals from the paper - stocky, pragmatic Bob Salas (Rispoli) and the wiry, unhinged Moberg (Ribisi). The latter's physicality is incredible, his body constantly fighting to stay balanced from taking so many drugs. He lopes through life, and even offers the occasional worthwhile contribution. But he's a guy who knows his days are numbered and is willing to spend the rest of them blazed out of his mind.

There are sequences that are memorable because they are simply outrageous: people blowing flames from high octane alcohol, two guys having to lap ride in order to drive a car; and then there's the loopy visit to a voodoo witch doctor. But what's remarkable about the film is exactly how unremarkable it is.

The velocity of Thompson's dialogue - some of it lifted verbatim from the novel – really needed visuals there were similarly larger than life. The muted color scheme and flat point-and-shoot style was probably a conscious choice, but it was the wrong one.

I never felt the heat of Puerto Rico, never felt the danger of untouchable millionaires, never cared during the out-of-nowhere sequence in which Chenault decides to stay and party in a potentially dangerous environment. *The Rum Diary* is a diamond in the rough, a potentially potent tale depicting one of America's most important voices, guided (and produced) by one of Hollywood's biggest stars, and it still just kind of sits there.

Maybe it's because *Fear and Loathing*, directed by Terry Gilliam, was presented in such a wildly-visceral way that this film suffers by comparison. Say what you will about Gilliam's colorful opus, but it's considered a modern classic.

Sure, it's divisive but so was Thompson.

And it was noteworthy enough to inspire one of the craftier visual jokes in the animated film *Rango* (2011). I doubt *The Rum Diary* will be similarly celebrated.

POSTSCRIPT:

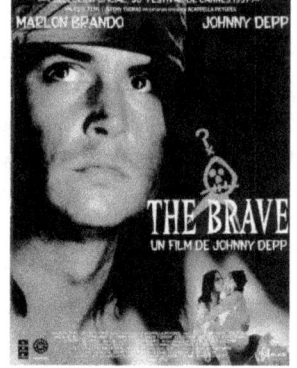

The Rum Diary was a worthy failure, an expensive labor of love that nobody wanted to see. It happens. But don't think Johnny Depp is immune to the mid-life career crisis. Oh no.

In 1997, Depp directed and starred in *The Brave*, a notoriously awful vanity project so bad, it was never even released in the states, either theatrically or on video. But fear not: the internet is your friend. *The Brave* is available online in its entirely, and really has to be seen in all of it's fetid glory, if for no other reason, to see Marlon Brando's completely insane wheelchair-bound soliloquy about snuff films. Go. Now. It's the reason the internet was created.

2 THE WAY THINGS SHOULD BE

...AND LOTS OF OTHER UNSOLICITED ADVICE.

On sports radio you hear the following term a lot: "Don't hate the player, hate the game." According to Urban Dictionary, it means: "Do not fault the successful participant in a flawed system; try instead to discern and rebuke that aspect of its organization which allows or encourages the behavior that has provoked your displeasure." I could not agree more.

I love movies, TV, music and books, but I'm not a fan of the businesses that distribute them. Art can illuminate, inspire, and act as a cultural hinge on which everything from style to public opinion can turn. Art is pure, motivated by the desire to create, arouse and transform.

However, the corporations which distribute said art might as well be selling widgets. More often than not, their model is built on the desire to simply make more money. Don't get me wrong: I do not begrudge businesses and corporations the ability to exist and thrive. In fact, art *needs* commerce, and vice versa.

But here's a quote from the first *Men in Black* film: "A person is smart. People are stupid." And when you are spending a hundred million dollars or more on your major Hollywood release, that is not the time to challenge your audience.

According to Hollywood bean counters, the dumber the film, the better. Why tell new jokes when you can recycle the same ones over and over again? Adam Sandler has built an entire career on that theory.

The mysterious soccer moms that make up the Motion Picture Association of America (MPAA) adhere to a list of criteria regarding boobies and curse words that's as inconsistent as it is dated.

Look no further than the 2012 public spat between the Weinstein Company and the MPAA over the initial R-rating given to their documentary *Bully*. The issue was six F-words, which apparently was four too many. The movie, geared toward teens, was eventually edited and released as a PG-13, but this was only the latest dust-up with an organization that all too often has missed the point.

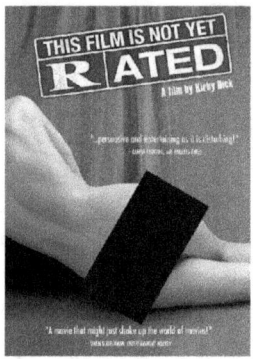

[NOTE: Check out Kirby Dick's excellent expose/documentary *This Film is Not Yet Rated*.]

Don't feel sorry for the studios. Because some number cruncher figured out that PG-13 movies are more profitable, you have scores of adult-oriented films watered down in post-production to be eligible for the lesser rating. The most egregious recent example of wanting to have it both ways was how Twentieth Century Fox handled both the production and the promotion for *Live Free or Die Hard* (2007).

And then there are the trailers, which are often produced by advertising agencies not invested in the actual filmmaking process. Hence, comedy trailers reveal all the best gags and action trailers, the biggest explosions.

Deadline Hollywood recently posted a report about how studios don't even care about revealing the entire film in the promos, so long as the opening weekend is as big as it can be.

Does it get any more cynical than that?

MPAA: The Real Slim Shady

September 20, 2000

WARNING: Contains profanity!

It's an election year and the politicians suddenly want to clean up Hollywood. The Director's Guild of America recently declared the long-standing ratings system antiquated, prompting MPAA president Jack Valenti to insist that system is just fine, thank you.

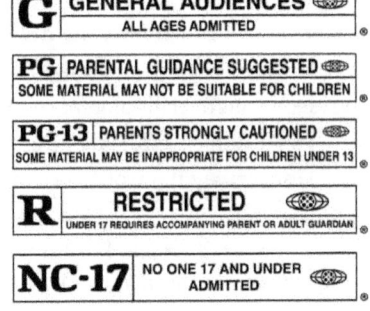

What gives? Is it the fact that Hollywood got caught with their hand in the post pubescent cookie jar, with all those recently-exposed memos about marketing adult fare to kids? Is it political jockeying or the natural reaction to a system that simply does not work anymore?

To answer that loaded question, one has to examine the history. When films became liberated in the 1960's, the Motion Picture Association of America introduced a content-based ratings system. The G, PG, R, X system worked fine until the early 1970's, when independent producers began dabbling in adult entertainment and appropriated the X rating.

Despite the fact that Hollywood awarded its Best Picture statue to *Midnight Cowboy*, an X-rated film, the stigma stuck, and X forever came to represent pornography. In 1990, the NC-17 was introduced, but nothing changed. The stigma remained, because many major newspapers and theater chains would not carry any association to NC-17 films.

It was the Hayes Code all over again. Look it up.

Eyes Wide Shut was released uncut everywhere but North America, where it had to be digitally-altered to get an R rating. And now the shocking - SHOCKING! - revelation that the big studios have targeted the all-important teen demographic with adult fare.

Yep, something sure has to give, and the best answer is to completely rethink the MPAA ratings system. Why? Because it's random and wildly inconsistent. Let's take Quentin Tarantino's preferred word of choice, the dreaded F-word. Despite the fact that its continued usage has dulled its effectiveness, it's still considered the heavyweight champion of colorful metaphors.

You'd think the MPAA guidelines would be clear, but examine the evidence: say the word once in a film ("Get the fuck down!") and we're talking PG-13. Use the word to describe a sex act, or as an insult, and we slide into R territory. But check out the PG-rated 1988 drama *Running on Empty* and you'll hear Judd Hirsch say the word at least a dozen times, but in the most general sense possible. Example: "He fucking did what?"

If one word (that everyone agrees is the harshest of the curse words) can yield so many different ratings possibilities, just imagine the hundreds of other mathematical combinations.

A hailstorm of bullets in a James Bond film is good for a PG-13, but spill blood once and it's an R. *The Nutty Professor II* features the comedic rape of a human from a giant hamster and got away with a PG-13, while the feel-good Julia Roberts drama *Erin Brockovich* was slapped with an R because of Erin's potty mouth. The violent *American Psycho* escaped an NC-17 by trimming a sex scene, but left all the graphic carnage intact.

None of it makes any sense, but until the MPAA creates a rating system that looks past counting bullets and F-words, the studios will continue to shamelessly exploit the loopholes.

In the center of all this bluster is the fact that British Board of Film Classification has just revamped their rating system, loosening up what falls into the 18 category and tightening up at the 12 level. Like the video game industry, the MPAA should adopt an age-based level of criteria and cap the limit at 18.

Let's face is, when kids can vote and join the military at 18, they should be able to watch whatever they want.

Films should fall into four distinct categories: G, for general audiences, PG for questionable content, 15 and 18. *Eyes Wide Shut* just might make an 18 while *Erin Brockovich* and *Armageddon* would qualify for 15. Directors could be free to express themselves without the studios dictating a prior rating for marketing's sake, and then they only culprits would be the filmmakers themselves.

But I'm having flights of fancy. The studios have cracked the code that PG-13 movies are more profitable but they fail to take a gander at what's happening on the music charts. Eminem has sold five million copies of his scathing and brilliant *The Marshall Mathers LP*. Critics love the album, parents hate it, but everyone's buying it and/or has an opinion about it.

Now imagine if Interscope Records had contractually bound Eminem to deliver a check-marked list of acceptable criteria. Like it or not, Eminem has sparked debate about hateful lyrics simply because he was not censored, and any dialogue between parents and kids can only be good.

When a celebrated action director like John Woo is contractually bound to deliver his *Mission: Impossible 2* at 135 minutes and PG-13 with little care from Paramount as to what the film's actually about, it's clear the tail is wagging the dog.

The rating comes first, the art second.

Yipee-Ki-Yay, Muffled Gunshot!

July 23, 2007

Have you ever watched a movie on TV and about a few minutes in, it occurred to you that something is off?

Sure, people are running around shooting at each other and the intensity is high, but it's all very sterile. The gunshots are loud and plaster and debris fly everywhere but then it occurs to you. Nobody's swearing. They aren't even talking much. And the sentences are clipped and choppy.

Then, you realize that you have a choice. You could continue watching a broadcast-friendly version or you can stop and wait for the real one, with the blood and the F-bombs. If you're a purist, you'd opt out right there. I certainly would.

But what if the very first version the studio gave us was the watered-down version and you didn't have a choice? To the bottom-liners at Twentieth Century Fox, who decided to shoehorn the 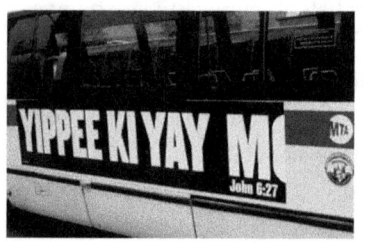 profane, violent R-rated *Live Free or Die Hard* into a family-friendly PG-13 package, I say this with love: fuck you very much.

Too harsh, you say? Not for a movie series in which the catch phrase is "Yippee Ki-yay, motherfucker!" The cynical bastards in Fox's promotion think tank even went so far to advertise their neutered action sequel on buses with the works "Yippee Ki-yay, Mo..."

Well, you can't accuse them of false advertising.

Why am I making such a big deal about this? Because this is a *Die Hard* movie, and if Fox had just been confident, the much-awaited R-rated action film would have seemed like a breath of fresh air in a summer filled with PG-13 product placement and CGI.

And because, frankly, a decent movie was compromised.

When I complained about the fact that Fox had recut *Live Free or Die Hard* to eliminate the F-bombs on my KGO segment, a nice (older) lady called in to ask what was so bad about having no profanity in a film?

Absolutely nothing, ma'am.

That is, until you notice the movie breaking into hives to try and cut around it ... until full exchanges are rendered so incomprehensible, they seem like something from *Grindhouse*, with missing parts ... until the editors have to re-use shots to cover bad looping and characters are seem waving their hands in the background but we cannot hear them.

And until you reach the single line of dialogue that everyone in the audience is waiting to hear and it sounds like this: "Yippi ki yay, mother fu(BANG)."

There is a really funny compilation of dubbed bits from *Die Hard 2*, in which the famous line is rendered "Yippee Ki Yay, Mister Falcon!" At least if they had used that line, it would have been satisfying in a meta sort of way, like director Len Wiseman saying to the world that this wasn't his idea, dammit.

Oh, and don't get me started on how the MPAA allowed *Gunner Palace* and *The Hip-Hop Project* to score the PG-13 despite rampant F-bombs - and we can't get one Yippee Ki Yay?

Live Free or Die Hard is a surprisingly solid entry in the series, the best since the first, and a complete updating of the adventures of John McClane that makes him relevant while proving how irrelevant he really is. It's really the only way to revisit this character 19 years after the original, and a road traveled well by the likes of Rocky Balboa.

That's why I'm so steamed about this. If *Live Free* had been just another craptastic sequel ala *Spider-man 3*, it would be bad no matter what the rating.

The stunt work (yes, by real humans) is impressive and Wiseman finally breaks through the CG ceiling that was hampering his work in the *Underworld* series. Everything in those films looked shiny and chintzy. *Die Hard* looks and feels like a tough world.

It also helps that Bruce Willis imbues his iconic role with all the grace notes you'd expect from this character at this age.

This is a John McClane that bears the scars of his past triumphs. Although not explicitly spelled out in the film, being a celebrity creates a lot of baggage that one's family has to deal with. Since saving his wife in the Nakatomi tower in 1988, this is a guy who has battled depression, alcoholism and watched his marriage end in divorce. Not the stuff of your typical shoot 'em up.

At the beginning of *Live Free or Die Hard*, McClane is staking out his grown daughter (Mary Elizabeth Winstead) to make sure her boyfriend doesn't get out of line. His gallantry results in her calling him an asshole. When he says, "I eat a lot of dinners alone," what he means is that being a hero ain't what it's cracked up to be.

His character is defined by being the wrong guy in the wrong place at the wrong time. But I think there is an argument for Willis being the right guy in the right role at the right time.

Being a *Die Hard* movie, there are terrorists, and as always, they are motivated by money. But as opposed to break into a building and take a few hostages, Thomas Gabriel (Timothy Olyphant) uses America's reliance on computer technology to enact a "fire sale," the three-part process of shutting America down. It's a juicy premise and once you get past the fact that a few strokes on a keyboard can open random doors or use cars as weapons by pointing them into a tunnel the wrong way, you're good to go.

Willis spends much of the film with Justin Long, who plays a hacker unwittingly involved in the fire sale. They have nice chemistry, with Long getting most of the better lines. A funny exchange about McClane's love of Credence Clearwater Revival perfectly captures the divide between young and old.

Kevin Smith appears as The Warlock, a thirtysomething hacker living in his mom's basement. Maggie Q is the badass (and at times, indestructible) girlfriend of Gabriel who delivers kung fu blows so brutal, you wonder how Willis can possibly overcome her. So, he finds a suitable weapon: his SUV.

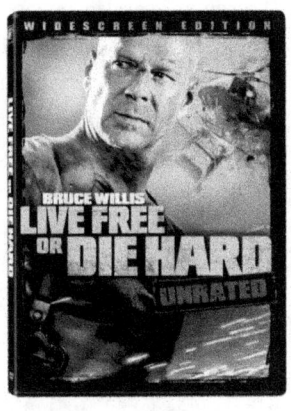

There are a few great sequences, not the least of which the aforementioned tunnel sequence (the one in which McClane kills a helicopter with a car), and a long suspenseful drive to the finale that features a crumbled freeway and a harrier jet. The *Die Hard* tradition of cat-and-mouse played over a walkie-talkie is alive and well, but enhanced with all the exposition a hacker can access.

But, to be fair, even without the rating controversy, there are still a few nits to pick. McClane smashes a car window that is intact after they steal the car. An OnStar operator is able to help even though all lines of communications have been cut. Why is every road jammed with traffic, except for the ones McClane travels on?

And what of the breakdown of civilization? *The Trigger Effect* told of the effects of a world relying on electricity and how quickly things devolve when people cannot communicate or get to an ATM. Wouldn't things break down that much faster a decade later?

But the mass hysteria, looting and desperation that would likely occur over many states in not even hinted at. It's a fascinating sociological angle that the movie completely misses. But if we were to nickel-and-dime every action movie for believability, we'd be missing the point.

The *Die Hard* series have always remained a cut above because of its heart. You care this poor beat-down son of a bitch. The *Lethal Weapon* series also began with an 80's classic that spawned three sequels, but as those films became bloated casts-of-thousands parodies, this fourth *Die Hard* movie features just two characters from the first - and one of those was a three-year-old girl.

But I'm digressing again, because I have to wait until Fox decides to release the Unrated DVD with the version we should have gotten in the first place. If they follow the release pattern of the similarly maligned *Alien Vs. Predator* (another film that was re-cut for a PG-13 even after being spawned by two R-rated series...), we'll get the real version a year after they make all they can off this one.

The last time I got so pissed off about studios treating us like babies was when the entire world got Stanley Kubrick's uncut *Eyes Wide Shut* but North America got the edited version. And I'm not alone: I would not be surprised if *Shut's* box office has suffered in the wake of this cinematic circumcision.

For now, we get a glimpse of what might have been. Against all odds, this improbable third *Die Hard* sequel delivers the goods. Well, most of them, at least.

Yippee ki yay.

The Matrix Fumbles The Ball

October 6, 1999

> **NOTE**: I realize that the inner-workings of the VHS-based video industry are about as relevant today as that of your average One Hour Photo employee. But I included this column as an example of exactly where the industry was at in 1999. VHS was dying, DVD was coming into prominence due to its low price and great quality, and the big studios had no idea what the hell to do.

Have you had a problem trying to rent *The Matrix*?

Amazon.com offers this simplified explanation for rental-priced titles: "Why is this video so expensive? It was priced by the studio for the rental market. The price often drops to under $30 within six months of its video release date."

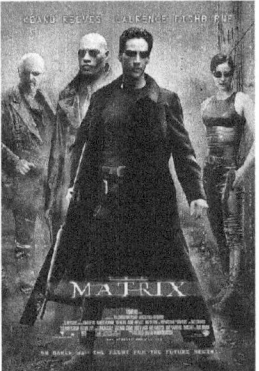

That's an understatement. After the surprise box office success of the Keanu Reeves sci-fi flick last Spring, you'd think Warner would have chosen to release the tape direct to sell-through, meaning the average Joe could pick it up for $19.95 or less.

But not only did Warner decide to go with the dreaded $106 rental price, they also foolishly announced they would be officially dropping the price to $14.95 by November 23rd.

That's a mere nine-week window for stores to make back the $78 distributor price at three bucks per rental. The usual rental-to-sale window is four to six months.

Warner thought they'd be able to drop over a million copies into the marketplace, but when retailers realized *The Matrix* had a rental life of just over two months, everybody backed off on their orders, including Big Blue, itself, Blockbuster.

The result was a less than spectacular 550,000 copies - hardly a record - and a big fat message to Warner Bros.

Because of Warner's greed, *The Matrix* will be impossible to rent for the next two or three weeks, but omnipresent in sell-off bins shortly thereafter.

The result was a lot of backpedaling on Warner's part. It dropped the stringent return requirements for stores who participate in revenue sharing and extended the rental window two weeks to December 7th. Now, when you visit Amazon.com, the only VHS listed is that December release.

Artisan Entertainment is taking the opposite approach with their breakthrough smash *The Blair Witch Project*, which touches down on video and DVD October 22nd, a week before Halloween and a scant three months after being released in theaters. Best yet, Artisan is selling the flick for $22.95 or less.

Artisan will ship five million copies, which will stimulate rentals and sales simultaneously. Both *The Matrix* and *Blair Witch* are adult-skewed R-rated titles, hardly the Disney fare you'd see in line at Safeway. But *Blair* will satisfy both sides of the coin, while *The Matrix* will continue to be a sore point for both studio and retailers.

By attempting to throw their weight around with their biggest title of the year, Warner tried to nab a bigger chunk of the pie and failed miserably.

For years, retailers have screamed for more sell-through pricing and an evenly-structured deal. Blockbuster and Hollywood Video get the breaks and the mom and pop stores get screwed. But this time, Warner tried to put the screws to everyone and it backfired.

Next time someone tells you that *The Matrix* is rented and hard to get, now you'll know why.

Trailer Trash

August 29, 2001

I'm not sure when it started. Maybe it was the trailer for *Speed*, in which preview audiences were shown the bus blowing up.

Movie trailers used to be an art form. The notion of capturing a tone and conveying a sense of concept without revealing too much is a tricky thing to do. But now trailers are like cliff's notes, or if you will, Movies For Dummies.

Welcome to the brave new world of trailers in which every plot point, great line of dialogue and surprising revelation is revealed in the two minute ad.

Those helpful promotional folks must know that we're a busy lot these days, so they make it helpful by making it so we don't have to sit through the whole movie.

Think I'm kidding? Stop reading right now if you don't like movie spoilers. Then again, if you watch television, you've probably seen everything I'm about to describe.

The trailer for *Cast Away* shows Tom Hanks getting trapped on an island, making a fire and doing a little dance afterward, growing a beard, and eventually going home, to which his ex, Helen Hunt, runs to him in the rain and tells him he's the love of her life. Oh, and also that he's been gone for four years, there was a funeral and he eventually winds up at a literal crossroads.

If you've seen the flick, they you know that was pretty much the whole movie. So, I ask you, why should anybody pay four bucks to rent, much less ten dollars to see this movie in a theater? Of course, the answer is that we shouldn't.

If the promo folks behind these ads think so little of their audience as to spoon feed the entire shebang, and people are growing increasingly steamed at trailers for this insulting practice, you'd think the public would respond by sending Hollywood a message. They did. *Cast Away* made $228 million at the box office.

The reason for this rant is Universal Home Video's ad campaign for *Hannibal*, which just came out on DVD. Granted, the movie made $165 million at the box office, but that doesn't mean that everyone know how it ends. As a film critic and overall fan of movies, I have been ever so careful in talking about Hannibal's parting shot to Clarice. It was a secret worth keeping.

The movie was definitely flawed and most of those flaws came from Thomas Harris' repugnant novel. The best parts of the movie were, of course, the scenes that had Hannibal Lecter and Clarice

Starling together in them. The new ending (different from the novel) was a delicious cinematic moment that, at once, cranked up the suspense, and introduced an extreme coda to Hannibal and Clarice's twisted relationship.

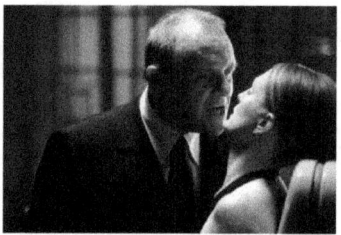

Hint: It had something to do with handcuffs and a meat cleaver.

What a way to end a movie!

To seemingly forever alter a main character and send the audience home debating whether Hannibal *really* did what he appeared to do. It was a masterstroke, especially considering how many things the film did wrong.

So imagine my surprise to realize one of the video ads is comprised entirely of that scene! The line is spoken, the cleaver comes down - WHACK! - Rent it tonight!

Have you ever had someone give away the ending of a movie to a friend and you just feel like smacking them? That's how I felt.

The identity of Keyser Soze, the switcheroo in *Fight Club*, the real meaning behind the line "I see dead people." These are moments that make the movie. These moments tap into the pure connection between the viewer and the film when an indelible impression is made forever.

Why would you want to rob somebody of that discovery? More importantly, why would a studio that's relying on your hard-earned dollars want to ruin the experience for you when their quarterly earnings and market share is on the line?

And it's not just a few movies, it's most of them: Ben Affleck crying while cradling a dead guy in the *Pearl Harbor* trailer, Matthew McConaughey chasing after Jennifer Lopez after telling her dad "I love your daughter," in the ad for *The Wedding Planner*. Even the trailer for *Jay and Silent Bob Strike Back*, which parodies Hollywood, reveals the best cameos.

In the season's one moment of restraint, Warner released *A.I. Artificial Intelligence* to a crowd that had no idea what to expect because of how vague the ads were, and most people didn't like it.

Think I'm making too much of this? Next time you're gonna tell somebody a joke, start with the punch line first and then double back and start from the beginning. Watch the person's face if it's a really long joke and see when they become irritated.

So what have we learned?

That despite the best interest of some to keep hidden those nuggets of the film-going experience, the studios will continue releasing trailers and TV commercials that reveal key points, shocking moments and all the biggest money shots; and that they don't care how many directors, actors, and common folk grouse about it.

Also, that as much as we complain, we still get in line, rent that video or buy that DVD.

In essence, that the joke's on us.

The Old-Fashioned Way

October 4, 2000

Last week, following years of intense lobbying by frustrated animators, the Academy of Motion Picture Arts and Sciences announced the creation of a new Oscar, for Best Animated Feature.

Too little, a little too late, guys.

In the past calendar year, Fox's *Titan A.E.* lost so much money that the studio abandoned all future productions and closed down the animation facility. Disney, as well, closed down production on a handful of future projects because of the costly disappointment that was *Dinosaur*, and the fact that the early word on *The Emperor's New Groove* isn't good.

I think it's safe to say that the animation boom of the 90's is over, and most of it will go unrecognized.

If the Academy had introduced this Oscar years ago, maybe Disney could boast four or five wins. Maybe the award synergy could have spilled into the other categories and Robin Williams may have actually snagged a nod for his manic work in *Aladdin*. Maybe *The Iron Giant* might not have unceremoniously limped to video.

With Warner Bros. and Fox out of the game, and Disney trying to second guess whether their audiences would prefer movies without singing teapots, the only real winner here is Pixar, the creators of *Toy Story*, and *A Bug's Life*. Pixar makes movies the old fashioned way: with story and characters higher on the priority list than dolls or lunchboxes. They let Disney worry about all that marketing stuff, leaving Pixar free to do what it does best, that is to make great movies.

Toy Story 2 was not only one of the best movies of 1999; it was also one of the best sequels ever, and currently the 16th biggest movie of all time. The winner of Best Comedy or Musical at the

Golden Globes, it couldn't come close to winning an Best Picture Oscar, even it had made Woody gay and gave Buzz a life-threatening disease with a Shakespearean accent.

Actually, the time is perfect for an animation category. With photo-realistic CGI actors headlining *Dungeons and Dragons* and the much-anticipated *Final Fantasy*, has anybody thought that the answer to an impending actor's strike could be found within the computer? Maybe all of Hollywood's top draws should sit down for a face scanning in the event this thing should drag on.

And speaking of those strikes, a few weeks ago, I commented about how the studios would most likely flood the market with re-mastered anniversary editions and director's cuts of classic films. Well, if Warner's test-run of 1973's *The Exorcist* is any indication, then let the strike begin tomorrow.

First and foremost, the print was beautiful, and as sharp as any 2000 release should look on the big screen. There are nuances that a 15-year old videotape could never reproduce, and director William Friedkin certainly had a way with actors.

To my amazement, the story of the ultimate battle between good and evil, over the soul of a young girl in Georgetown actually took its time telling the story. There were no thrill ride bumpers anywhere to be found: only rich, detailed characterizations that were allowed to breathe without cutting away every four seconds.

Jason Miller as the confused, faith-challenged Father Damien Karras is simply one of the best debut performances in the history of film, and he was justly nominated. Linda Blair (with the vocal assistance of Mercedes McCambridge) equally captured one of the most affecting portraits of evil, and one that has never been equaled.

The Exorcist has been technically surpassed in many ways over the years: performances have become more vivid, special effects more gory and over-the-top. But the reason it still dazzles in 2000 is because once upon a time, movies had believable three-dimensional characters that inspired thoughtful performances.

It dares to show us explorations of faith, disillusionment and people who dare to be human. That kind of approach to big-ticket thrills is virtually extinct in the current model for what makes a film successful today. And yet, *The Exorcist* made $8.5 million on 669 screens, and will continue to expand, based on its popularity.

I hope Hollywood will learn one thing: that there's money in them thar re-releases, and continue to mine the vaults for modern classics to re-master.

And that's not such a bad thing either.

POSTSCRIPT:

It's fascinating how much animation has changed in one decade. This column depicted the entire art form as suffering from financial

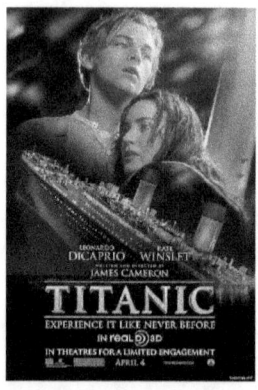

woes and technology that wasn't quite there yet. But by 2010, Pixar had delivered a handful of profitable classics (*Cars, Wall-E, Ratatouille, Up, Toy Story 3*) and had influenced the entire genre with its "story first" approach and striking 3D effects. *Despicable Me, Cloudy with a Chance of Meatballs* and *How to Train Your Dragon* are prime examples of CG-animation done at the highest level. 3D is also responsible for the proliferation of successful re-releases. Granted, you have to pay the premium ticket price and watch something converted from 2D, but it's allowed us the chance to see Disney classics such as *The Lion King* and *Beauty and the Beast,* and live action epics like *Titanic* and the *Star Wars* films on the big screen again. You take the good with the bad.

Kill your Darlings

November 10, 1999

It's funny, how people react to change. They seem to roll with the events of their own lives better than those of fictional lives.

Or fictional deaths.

Kill off a beloved character and prepare for the wrath of rabid fandom. The soaps casually walk this line all the time. A character dies and audiences tune in for the funeral. But, as soon as the actor strikes out on the big screen, that character might experience a rebirth that would make Spock proud.

Think Bobby Ewing in the shower. Nuff said.

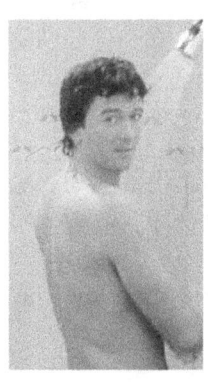 How many times can Robin die in the *Batman* comics? How many times can the U.S.S. Enterprise blow up or crash? How often can Neve Campbell escape Ghost-face in the *Scream* series? I hope not for very much longer.

Of course, when producers try to shake up the mixture, it's generally too little, too late. *Star Trek* bungled the death of James T. Kirk so badly, that his alter-ego William Shatner revived him in a series of popular books; *Lois and Clark's* nuptials were such a crock, that loyal viewers had flown away by the time they really did the deed. And everyone's been waiting so long for Mulder and Scully to kiss, their coupling may be, ahem, anti-climatic.

So what's a good writer of hero fiction to do? Let the journey take its own course. To keep a character alive simply to continue a financial venture is crass and goes against the integrity of the piece. Such might have been the case in the series of published *Star Wars* sequels, until recently.

R.A. Salvatore's novel *The New Jedi Order: Vector Prime*, has incurred the wrath of fans by - SPOILER ALERT - killing off a major character, and a good guy no less.

If you haven't heard who dies, I'm not gonna tell you, but the idea apparently came from George Lucas, himself. *Star Wars* sequel books have hopped all over an intricate canon of events, so any writer who pens a tale *after* the time depicted in this lineage, will be forced to adhere to a smaller galaxy far, far away.

Of course, the fans are responding as if someone was throwing bantha poo-doo at them.

Heroism and tragedy march valiantly into battle hand-in-hand. If literary characters are to grow at all, they must have life experiences. But the self-feeding Hollywood product of the past decade has watered-down the notion of personal growth. At the start of a new book or movie, nobody has any new scars or limps. It's as if time has stopped and reset in a perfect *Groundhog Day* sort of way.

The irony is that as much people piss and moan, these are the episodes that further their legacies. Would Picard's battle against the Borg been half as interesting had he not lost once before? Say the words "Gwen Stacy" to a die-hard Spider-man fan and it can only refer to her untimely death at the hands of the Green Goblin.

So I say, let 'em crash!

Let Scully have to grapple with being pregnant. Let Martin Riggs take his final bullet saving Roger Murtaugh. Let Rambo twist his ankle and hobble through the rest of the flick.

And let *Star Wars* characters die with dignity.

Besides, if it doesn't work out, maybe his cells can be regenerated on the Genesis planet.

Wait, that's been done already.

Oscar the Grouch: Crash vs. Brokeback Mountain
February 20, 2006

In September, nobody had any idea what the big Oscar juggernauts would be, especially since the Miramax era (in which movies were developed with the *intent* of winning Best Picture) is now over.

By December, a clearer picture had emerged but it's not until the guilds named their picks that true Oscar momentum begins. The only problem with that is that by the time the actual Oscar broadcast airs, there is so much buzz for the heirs apparent that it seems that nobody else could *possibly* win a given award.

And that makes for a boring Oscar telecast.

You can track that to when the Academy rescheduled the show to air a month earlier in the season (from March to February). By removing that important final month of campaigning and shifting momentum, surprises are virtually null and void now. The winners have already won their share of pre-award guild (DGA, Screen Actors Guild, etc.) and Golden Globe trophies, so there is no shock or awe when they win anymore.

By the time Jamie Foxx finally won his Oscar, I'd already heard his acceptance speech twice before. And that shocking Michael Moore tirade a few years back? Moore said the same exact speech the night before when he won the Independent Spirit Award.

So predictable are this year's awards that it would be a bigger shock if *Brokeback Mountain* DIDN'T win Best Picture. But I'll get to that in a minute.

Remove the surprises and what do you have? Good movies rewarded for their artistic merit, right? Sure, but the suits at ABC and the major studios aren't thinking about that. They are concerned that no Oscar contender has made over $100 million and that with no *Titanic* or *Lord of the Rings* in the race, nobody will have a movie to root for. Hence, low ratings again.

Well, whose fault is that? Now more than ever, there is a Grand Canyon between the crappy McMovies that win the box office every weekend and the good films that nobody really want to see anyway. High concept slop is fed to the masses with massive advertising blitzes, and the quiet, really great films go largely unnoticed.

Until, of course, they are nominated for awards.

Thanks to the award season, people now know what Phillip

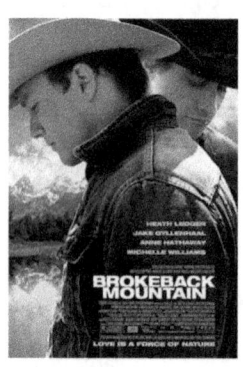

Seymour Hoffman's name is now, as opposed that "it's that creepy guy again." People suddenly realize that Reese Witherspoon can play other roles than romantic comedy leads. And it is sorta fun watching the look on someone's face when you ask if they've seen *Brokeback Mountain*.

If nothing else, this Oscar season has forced everyone to confront their own varying degrees of cultural tolerance, which is why it's fascinating that the two front-runners have become *Crash* and *Brokeback Mountain*. One asks a lot of hard questions and forces you to go inward to find the answers that best suit yourself. The other asks nothing but to be accepted as a simple, tragic love story, which in and of itself, is asking a lot.

Brokeback has been the front-runner the entire season, and I'm positive Ang Lee will win Best Director. But momentum has shifted for *Crash*, Paul Haggis' epic racism fable that doesn't lend itself to internet parodies as easily as the "gay cowboy" movie. There is a lot of whispering about how straight Academy voters really don't want to see *Brokeback Mountain* and are voting for it because "it's going to win, anyway."

To those who have asked me if I honestly think there should even BE a movie like *Brokeback Mountain* (and believe me, they have), my answer is this: Yes, as much as there should have been a movie called "*Guess Who's Coming To Dinner*" in the 60's. It's time. Let's move on and ask ourselves a more pertinent question: Which phobia is the most award-friendly? Homophobia or xenophobia?

The Academy is a group made up of 5,000 voters. They like to *see* actors acting, which is why showy performances win over subtlety every time. *Acting* gay is considered risky (and rewarded justly) but actually *being* gay counts against you.

The Hollywood community is often bashed for their outspokenness, and yet idolized at the magazine rack. Conservatism lords over what projects are green lit, yet anytime the neo-cons want to question flagging morals, they point to "Hollywood."

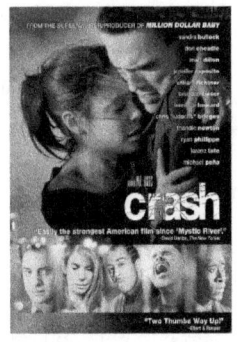

In other words, the Oscars are the perfect storm of politics, box office, buzz, paybacks, quality, advancements, tributes, fashion and good old-fashioned excitement about the flickering image on the movie screen. And in the end, it's all about the movies. And this is the Super Bowl of movies.

The Academy of arts and sciences created the Academy Awards to reward films that furthered the art of motion picture storytelling. And yet, the films that have won recently have furthered video sales more than artistic merit.

So, for me, the hardened critic, it's a breath of fresh air to see passionate, literate movies like *Brokeback Mountain, Crash, Capote, Good Night and Good Luck* and *Syriana* going to the playoffs.

3 RIPPED FROM THE HEADLINES

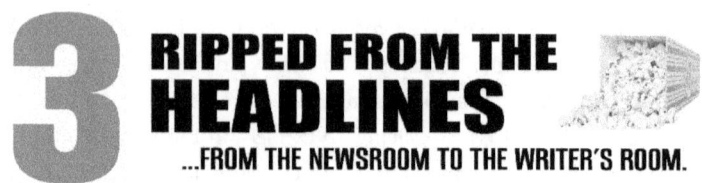

...FROM THE NEWSROOM TO THE WRITER'S ROOM.

"Can we film the operation? Is the head dead yet?
You know, the boys in the newsroom got a running bet.
Get the widow on the set. We need dirty laundry..."
                                        -Don Henley, "Dirty Laundry"

For many people, it has become a ritual to turn on the evening news and catch up on the stories of the day. In very rare instances, world-changing events make everybody lean forward and take note, but most times, the news is filled with garden variety political struggles, disappearances, and dog maulings.

Please know, I do not mean to be insensitive.

As much as I rage against the machine, I do so in the defense of those exploited by it. I can only imagine the personal horrors some of these poor folks must go through, and it is for that reason alone than I do not rubberneck.

People throw around the word "rape" and even go so far to use it as a cultural punch-line *("George Lucas raped my childhood!")*, but how else can you describe going through the most unimaginable personal disaster and having some TV reporter stick a camera in your face and ask you how you feel about it?

To be fair to the reporters, what a tough gig!

Full disclosure: I have a good many friends who work in the news industry, and just about every one of them is hard-working, good-hearted and takes pride in their work. They don't come to work with the intent of exploiting people. But then again, I work at a radio station that has been a model example on how to play fair.

No, I'm talking about TV news, especially those tasked with hourly newscasts, or worse, a 24-hour cycle. And in the end, it's all about the ratings and the commercial ad revenue for the bean counters upstairs.

Once again, don't hate the player, hate the game.

Having said all of that, there is no greater source of storytelling drama than our own experiences. Experts tell us to talk about our problems, and it has been through the exploration of said personal horrors that incredible works of art have emerged for centuries.

The movies are no different. From *Titanic* to *Roots*, from *Gone with the Wind* to *The Hurt Locker*, and even all three network movies about the Long Island Madam that aired days apart, people love watching stories about real people.

The best examples of "ripped from the headlines" do so by incorporating an event into an already existing world, say *Law and Order*. But the bigger the events, the more potential for varied perspectives. Count the number of movies based on the Vietnam or Iraq wars and we'd be sitting here for quite some time.

As a writer, I try to be as honest as I can, and as much as I loathe the sensationalism and exploitation of tragedy, I am not completely heartless.

Like many others, I have found writing to be therapeutic, especially in the wake of a major disaster or story that has affected me in some personal way.

And I'm the first to admit that profound global events have created moments of unforgettable cinema.

September 11, 2001

September 19, 2001

Hollywood be damned, we've seen this plot before. But Bruce Willis didn't save the day this time, as much as we hoped he would.

When the credits rolled on this one, all of the clichés came true. Our innocence was lost (again), our nightmares came true and in the end, nothing would ever be the same.

But beyond these oft-repeated phrases, what words could possibly capture the waves that continue to sweep the nation?

There are none.

Hollywood was very quick to compensate for the sudden shift in mood. Arnold Schwarzenegger's movie *Collateral Damage* was delayed because of its plot about terrorists destroying a building (and Arnie's family). The romantic comedy *Sidewalks of New York* didn't seen very funny anymore. Barry Sonnenfeld's *Big Trouble*, with an ensemble featuring Tim Allen concerns itself with a bomb smuggled onto an airplane.

Remember that hilarious scene in *Meet The Parents*, in which Ben Stiller did his bomb on an airplane routine - "bombombom, bombom-buh-bomb."

Funny a year ago. Not anymore.

Even the very cool *Spider-man* trailer that ended with a shot of a helicopter stuck in a web between the two World Trade Center towers is a tragically moot point. It too has been recalled and rethought.

But how far should Hollywood take this? Should every film that features the twin towers have those scenes altered? How can any film or TV show set in New York *not* deal with this?

How can the gang from *Friends* discuss anything else while sitting around Central Perk? Certainly the guys at *NYPD Blue* must have known some of the firefighters who lost their lives. And what of President Bartlet's administration on *The West Wing*?

I bring up these points to illuminate the truth as Hollywood simply must see it. September 11th happened. It's history now. Everything set before is a period piece, everything after is a new reality.

Is a television show that includes those horrific events guilty of exploitation, or is it a form of healing? I think it can be the latter. People have poured into blood banks and hung flags because of the overwhelming desire to do something, *anything*. It's all we can do to not feel overwhelmed.

Just as Mister Rogers took to the airwaves to comfort kids in the wake of John F. Kennedy's assassination, Ross and Rachel's ability to help bring people through this should not be underestimated.

The news media, for its part, has provided a curious mix of the accurate and the sensational, the shocking and the soothing, and the stories. Oh, the stories. These accounts of lost loved ones, heroic deeds, and final cell phone calls cut deeper than the visuals of planes and explosions.

We've seen the explosions in movies. But these stories speak of everyone we've ever met, and everyone we care about. My wife is a flight attendant for United and I can't imagine what it must have been like for her to get back on a plane again.

But she got on with her life, as must we all.

How we respond to situations define who we are. To the countless who have donated blood, battled through the rescue and search operations, hung flags in support of the United States, or even the people who have leant an ear to those who grieve. You are the symbol of America, because you all have the freedom to choose your response. And you choose to help.

But there are the others: the kinds of scumbags that think it's funny to phone in bogus bomb threats or survivor reports; or to call people asking for fake donations; or those who think it's productive to vent their frustration against the Arab-Americans who live here. Needless to say, they're making things worse and helping those who hope to divide and conquer.

The news media has become a necessary evil. The networks have sought to provide what they can, sans commercials. But after excellent visual coverage of the initial attacks, once information became thin, it was back to business.

Why is it that reporters feel like they always have to have something to say? Even while KRON observed last Friday's minute of silence with exactly that, KPIX's news anchors covered the silence by babbling through it.

Within one day, we went from a nation divided after a bitter election to one united under the leadership of one government and a resurgence of patriotism. Everything is trivial now, from movies to sports to Monica Lewinsky.

But rest assured, once all of this dies down, Hollywood will be back to bringing us square-jawed heroes making sure terrorists pay for what they did.

Even after the networks yanked airings of *Independence Day* and the like, the nation's video stores filled up with people seeking action movies in which terrorists got theirs. We need some sort of closure, even if it does come from Bruce Willis or Will Smith.

Fahrenheit: Less is Moore

July 28, 2004

Let's talk politics.

But not the way most people do. Let's face it, 99% of all political debate among us non-political types boil down to "This is why I'm right, this is why *you're wrong*." With the country so polarized since the 2000 election, it's not just a conversation anymore, it's insulting.

The left looks at the right like they are all goose-stepping Fox News zombies. The right looks at the left like they are America-hating commies. Somewhere, in the middle, there has to be something that's um, fair and balanced?

No? Okay, how about at least informative. I'm an educated guy. I do a little thing like form my own opinions, which I have to admit, is a bit exhausting at times. You have to look hard because that facts are everywhere and nowhere at the same time.

In this highly-charged environment, everyone with a microphone or opinion will claim to have the answers and will remind you that you are ignorant if you don't agree with them.

I stayed out of the *Fahrenheit 9/11* debate for a good month before seeing it on the very day it became the first documentary to cross the $100 million mark. It was a Saturday night and unlike the party atmosphere during the organized initial sell-outs, this was a somber crowd, with very few instances of cheering or laughter.

People left the theater stone-faced. Gears were turning. And if *Fahrenheit 9/11* does nothing more than get people talking, then it's done its job.

And for the record - because you sort of have to preface your argument with your position these days - my opinion of Michael Moore is that he is a talented and compelling filmmaker who simply doesn't know when to fold 'em. All too often, he goes for the easy laugh, generally to point out how stupid someone is, punctuated with a banjo track.

If I wanted to laugh at stupid people, I'd just watch the Paris Hilton TV show. But laughing at stupid people sells tickets. And let's face it, there's a reason why *Bowling For Columbine* (a documentary!) won the Writer's Guild Best Screenplay Award.

When the president is told about the World Trade Center attack in that classroom, a montage shows a clock counting up to seven minutes afterward. Why should I believe that seven minutes passed, just because Moore shows us a clock? Hey, this is a guy who was shown talking to Charleton Heston about a dead girl long after Heston had already left.

But being disappointed by those types of narrative short-cuts in

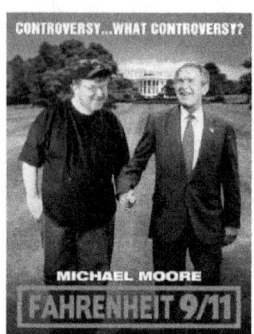

a Michael Moore movie would be like calling *Star Trek* unbelievable because you can hear sound in space. You just sort of take the leap.

Moore caught a lot of flak for playing his facts loose in *Columbine* and *Fahrenheit* still features Moore's thought bubble musings the way we speak for our pets to entertain fellow humans.

I'm not picking on Moore because I don't respect his politics or even his filmmaking abilities. In fact, I think he's one of the only unique voices not owned by a bigger conglomerate. So long as there is a Fox News, there needs to be a Michael Moore.

More times than not, I land on his side of the argument and applaud the fact that he is as dogged and fearless as any public figure I've ever seen. I just don't appreciate being manipulated when all you had to do was give me the facts.

Fahrenheit 9/11 is not fair and balanced. Michael Moore makes no attempt to hide his feelings about George W. Bush. What follows is a scattered narrative that connects the dots between Bush's doctored military records, the Bush and bin Laden family business connections and Moore's version of why we really went to war with Iraq. If you discount the cheap shots and oakie music, there is still no denying that this groundbreaking film offers a glimpse of the Bush administration through official records and B-roll video footage that is not generally served up on Fox News.

Much of the information on display has apparently been out there for years, but what I found fascinating, and particularly damning, are the words of those concerned, from their own mouths.

That footage of Bush in the classroom might have been played for laughs, but the underlying message was about the president's absolute paralysis without people around to tell him what to do. We may get the presidential sound bytes on the six o'clock news but once you open up that footage to show what happens before and after the money shot is quite revealing.

Oh, and for a media savvy group like, um, the administration, you'd think someone would have explained the basic principals of how a satellite feed works: once the camera is pointed at you, you're live even before you go live. Deputy Defense Secretary Paul Wolfowitz slobbering into his comb before sheepishly running it through his hair is a moment I wish I'd never seen. George W. making stupid, childish faces moments before addressing the nation on our war against terrorism is something I'm thankful to have. This and other visuals fly in the face of a very cultivated image.

These people should know better.

Dubya has never been accused of being a brilliant speaker, but there are candid moments that would have his biggest supporters heading out for popcorn. He bungles quotes, can never find the right words and frankly, looks like he'd be challenged to tie his own shoes. His administration is shown repeatedly contradicting themselves and Moore is too happy to run those clips side by side.

The much-debated Patriot Act becomes a subplot. We see the haphazard ways that the CIA has investigated average citizens for simply making conversation or trying to get breast milk through an airport but the movie shows us that having lighters on a plane is allowed, even following Richard "the shoe bomber" Reed. In classic Moore fashion, he points out that national security takes a back seat to the tobacco industry, whose sales would certainly be affected if passengers could not light right up after getting off a plane.

That's great stuff, but Moore drops the ball right before the goal line. After the jaw-dropping revelation that the Patriot Act was printed in the middle of the night to be voted on in the morning, and that hardly any of the senators actually read the bills they vote on, Moore the actor gets onto an ice cream truck to read the Patriot Act to the politicians. Moore the filmmaker never lets us hear any of the freedom-stripping text, but instead cuts away to something else.

Say what you will about Michael Moore but the guy has crafted a work that has sold $100 million worth of tickets and has played to every demographic. The initial wave was not unlike a protest rally. People were united in their anti-Bush fervor and scored the movie a record $21 million during its opening weekend.

But to suggest the box office response is a result of excited Democrats would be selling this audience short. People are curious, which is why the film will make six times its initial weekend, domestically. Comparatively, *Spider-Man 2* would have to make around $750 million to sustain that kind of momentum.

Michael Moore has created a new form of expression: the protest movie. Film history will look at this film as the first of its kind. In the near future, politics, scandals and culture will be debated through these cinematic polemics. And that includes the satire *Michael Moore Hates America.*

Fahrenheit 9/11 is nowhere as focused as *Bowling For Columbine* and actually feels pretty rushed at times. It will not be viewed as his best film and might actually fade away as soon as the election is over. In light of the anti-Murdoch documentary *Outfoxed* and Moore's own incendiary website, I was a bit underwhelmed.

But once the dust settles and opinions fade away, we are left with lingering visuals and unanswered questions that Moore is smart enough not to answer. When the credits roll, the feeling is one of uneasiness, like we've just scratched the surface of something that might end up being ugly.

If Michael Moore hadn't made this film now, Oliver Stone might have later. *Fahrenheit 9/11* is not unlike Stone's *JFK* in that it's impossible to watch either film without wondering how much we really don't know.

POSTSCRIPT:

How odd to think that, in 2004, Oliver Stone still had the reputation of a maverick! After all, this is the same filmmaker who would give us the melodramatic *World Trade Center* (2006), depicting the events of that horrible day with the enthusiasm of a TV movie, and follow that up with *W.* (2008), a "greatest hits" biopic about the (then) sitting president that asked no challenging questions whatsoever. Even when he returned to his own *Wall Street* sequel in 2010, a movie that unfolds against the financial crisis of 2008, the one-time provocateur was more interested in telling a father-daughter tale.

Pearl Harbor, the Movie. Thanks, Titanic!

May 11, 2001

In two weeks, Disney will release one of the most anticipated films of the year, the $135 million opus *Pearl Harbor*.

The tent-pole flick, set for release Memorial Day weekend, is a risky venture, but the Mouse House is setting up a few safeguards that aren't being sold to the American public alongside Ben Affleck and that money shot of the dropping bomb.

Pearl Harbor is a movie cut from the *Titanic* mold: a fictional love story set against a real-life historical event, with a huge budget and showy special effects. *Titanic* made over $1.8 billion at the box office, and won 11 Academy Awards including Best Picture. But before *Pearl Harbor* can pick up its Oscar statue, it's got some dicey waters to sail through.

First of all, the 2 hour, 50 minute epic has the biggest budget ever greenlit by a major studio. To get the film made, all of the key players agreed to work for scale. In the event the film actually makes a profit, everybody wins.

The other stumbling blocks are the filmmakers: producer Jerry Bruckheimer and director Michael Bay have shared success on two other Disney actioners: *The Rock* and *Armageddon*, but even if *Pearl* earns what the latter did; it's still not enough.

I'll be the first to admit that despite my better judgment, Bruckheimer's hyped-up rapid-fire cutting style and dumbed-down action has it's place in any given summer movie line-up *Gone In 60 Seconds*, anyone?). There's fine cuisine and there's popcorn. These guys make popcorn, and that's okay.

But the story of *Pearl Harbor* demands a little more reverence and dignity then, say, an asteroid flick with an Aerosmith soundtrack. If *Pearl Harbor* looks like a music video and is packed with dumb one-liners and crass sentimentality, you can expect an outcry from the purists.

All of these factors make the sport of tracking a film like *Pearl Harbor* fun for the market watchers. The risks are so high, the rewards so sweet, that the story of getting this film made and into theatres is, in many ways, much more exciting. History books can teach us what happened at Pearl Harbor, but the reverberations from this one movie can be history in the making.

That's what scares me.

Several movie-oriented websites are already posting reports about the demands Disney is putting on the theaters. In one case, a theater employee confirmed Disney is demanding the film screen on four of their ten screens, MUST put it in the four largest auditoriums, and KEEP it on those screens for 3 weeks.

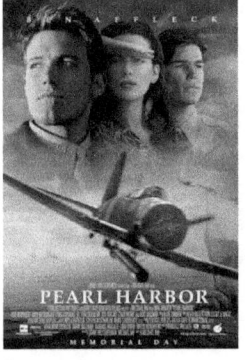

It gets worse.

Allegedly, Disney is also telling theaters specifically WHEN they should show the movie. In the case of the theater employee, show times start on the hour, every hour, from 11 am to 11 pm. If we don't comply with these rules then there's an excellent chance that we'll lose it to our competitors. If the theater isn't usually open past a certain point, they are now.

Another scooper confirms the demands, adding that it assures that *Pearl Harbor* will have the biggest auditorium in any given multiplex until June 29th and one of the larger ones until July 4th. So if your multiplex gets *Pearl Harbor* on May 25th, your dreams of seeing *Moulin Rouge, What's The Worst That Could Happen, The*

Animal, Evolution, Swordfish, Tomb Raider ,Dr. Doolittle 2, or *The Fast & The Furious* on the biggest screen will probably be for naught.

LucasFilm and Twentieth Century Fox made demands on *Star Wars, Episode I* but stopped short of issuing showtimes and hours of operation. Unlike *Star Wars* (which was privately financed by George Lucas), Disney has a lot to lose and they are stacking the deck to make sure people don't accidentally look past *Pearl Harbor*.

If these reports are true, and Disney is essentially bullying the theater owners into a shotgun wedding, *Pearl Harbor* could set a very dangerous precedent for big-budget films of the future. You think other studios won't begin demanding more screen time and perks? Play our movie for two months on these biggest screens or you lose out on the next big franchise film.

To the movie-goer, the endless sea of screens playing *Pearl Harbor* will mean that it's easy to catch the flick any time of the day. But the bean counters are failing to take into consideration what the big picture means. At this level of exposure, *Pearl Harbor* won't be an event film to wait in line for, and will certainly peak before those windows are up.

By mid-June, audiences will be on to *Tomb Raider* or any other of the summer's big guns (including Disney's own *Atlantis: The Lost Empire*, which leaves a lot of big screen still showing *Pearl Harbor*.

If *Pearl Harbor* emerges a box office hit, it won't be because the movie struck a nerve with an adoring public. But then there's also the possibility the movie will flop and theater owners have to sit on the thing for four weeks while the rest of the summer movie season opens around them.

For those distributors, May 25th might truly become the day that lives in infamy.

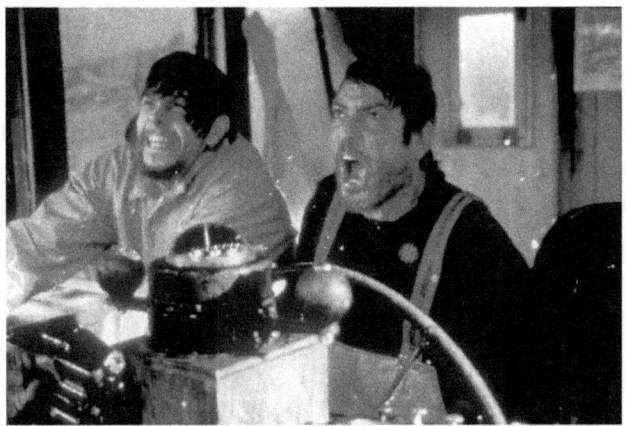

A Perfect Mess
July 5, 2000

I should have known going in. A Warner Bros. summer movie about the weather could mean only one thing: *Twister*.

For those who felt the same way about that 1996 plotless wonder as I did, then let this serve as a warning: *The Perfect Storm* is *Twister* without the flying cow.

All you're left with is stereotyped humans, oversimplified mumbo jumbo about storms colliding, and dialogue with gems like "You're heading right into the belly of the monster!"

Then again, there were a lot of folks who liked *Twister*. And Warner Bros. has rolled the $125 million dice that there's going to be a lot of folks willing to pay eight bucks to see that big-ass wave from the trailer. To those folks, I offer this public service announcement. Don't be afraid to arrive late. The money shot happens ten minutes before the end of its 135-minute running time.

The Perfect Storm is based on the actual 1991 occurrence of three massive weather systems moving headlong into one another and the poor bastard sword fishermen stuck in the middle on the ill-fated Andrea Gale.

Since it's a true story, let me say that I wish not to disgrace the memory of the hard working individuals who encountered Mother Nature in all her PMS'ing glory. It's just that you may find yourself wondering, as I did, who exactly was around to take notes during intimate moments of duress and heroics.

The book, Sebastian Junger's *The Perfect Storm: A True Story of Men Against the Sea* makes no such mistakes. Junger freely admits that it's impossible to know exactly how the Andrea Gail sank. Instead, the author paints a picture with first-hand accounts, character witnesses and the rescue of the three people caught in a sailboat, and rescued by the Coast Guard.

On paper, this analogy makes perfect sense. On film, such a comparison is lost because the movie tells us that what we are seeing is a true story, but we are never given any reason to care about why 30 minutes of screen time is spent following these three.

By the time the credits rolled, I wondered what the hell had just happened. Finding and reading parts of Junger's book certainly helped, but I didn't have to go back and read *Schindler's List* to understand what was happening there.

Wolfgang Peterson staffed his earnest adventure with a solid cast, but the script, loosely based on Junger's novel, didn't give them much to work with. George Clooney does want he can. It must have pained him coming off *Three Kings* and *Out Of Sight* to be saddled with dialogue so on the nose and perfunctory, it sounds ripped from one of those ripped-from-the-headlines movies of the week. That scowl probably wasn't from not being able to catch fish.

Money is the motivation for Clooney's Captain Billy Tyne to turn back around after an underwhelming catch, one that results in a smaller-than-expected paycheck for Mark Wahlberg's earnest

Bobby Shatford. Soon enough, everybody realizes that a turnaround is in the air, so they party hard one night (in which everyone's back story is clumsily laid out for us) before heading back out.

An early indication of the overwrought tone crafted by the usually dependable Peterson is how much weight the entire town seems to put on these guys simply headed back out to sea, something they do all the time. As one character ominously predicts, "I just got a bad feeling about this." Yeah, no kidding.

You'd think a damned asteroid was going to destroy the world if they didn't succeed in catching some more fish. There's so much dismay and fretting, I wondered if these poor guys got treated that way every time they headed out off to work. I mean, come on--it's not like they're dismantling a leaking nuclear plant. I'd spend a lot of time at the local pub if that were the case, too.

The storm takes a good hour of screen time to brew. By then, we've met George's cantankerous (but lovable) crew, survived a mini-storm, a surprise shark attack and absolutely no character development whatsoever, save for Captain George's desire to catch fish because that's what he does.

Without first telling his crew, the good skipper heads into deeper waters and they catch mountains of fish. This makes the crew happy. We know this because all of them - even the ones who wanted to kill each other earlier - are grinning ear to ear. *The Perfect Storm* has no less than four sequences that depict a happy crew gutting rubber swordfish, and packing them on ice.

At least *Twister*, ludicrous as it was, was a good-looking movie. *The Perfect Storm* spends a fair amount of time in calm water, which means lots and lots of bad computer generated water effects just beyond the parameter of an obviously indoor set with a wave machine. Once the storms actually start, then it's overkill, with almost every shot featuring a wave crashing down upon our heroes as their boat is throttled.

To be fair, there are a handful of great special effects, but most of them are vast ocean shots with the waves swelling. And then there's that poster image wave, which is, by all accounts the showstopper. It's a shame that Warner Bros. decided to put that in the trailer, but after seeing the film, it was probably their best card. It's not like the memorable dialogue was gonna pack people in.

The Perfect Storm even gets the angle wrong. So much time is spent on the boat with these guys, you'd think the story was actually about them. It's not. The recurring theme is the effect men of industry have on the loved ones around them, and how our passions can kill us.

A least, that's what the film should have been saying, but instead, poor Diane Lane has to carry the entire anti-establishment arc on her little shoulders, complaining and crying to boyfriend Wahlberg how much she doesn't want him to go, and then fretting and crying once he has.

There is no satisfactory conclusion to this movie, and once the credits roll, you realize that Mother Nature wasn't the villain after all. Once again, someone in upper management is banking on the fact that American audiences are attracted to the bad things that happen to common folk, and hoping that a few cool special effects shots in the trailer will disguise the fact that at its core, *The Perfect Storm* is a soulless machine, as exploitative as *Hard Copy*, and as manipulative as an episode of *VH1: Behind The Music*.

I'd like to think a flying cow might have made the difference, but I seriously doubt it.

Trenchcoat Mafia: The Motion Picture

April 28, 1999

Last Tuesday, the world watched the Columbine High School tragedy unfold, live on television and the ratings soared. By Wednesday, the entertainment industry was breaking a sweat to find ways to feel the pain of those affected by the school shootings.

Ironically, the title of the *Rockford Files* TV-movie that aired that night summed it up best - *If It Bleeds, It Leads*. No kidding. CNN was up 283 percent, Fox News scored its biggest numbers in its history, and MSNBC was up more than 200 percent. A special edition of NBC's Dateline at 10 p.m. Tuesday, which was devoted entirely to the Colorado tragedy, wound up as the most-watched show of the night, drawing 14.5 million viewers.

In the days following, CBS showed the most restraint. The tiffany network pulled an episode of *Promised Land* which depicted a similar event, and aired an episode of *60 Minutes II*, which was about something else entirely. But on the other networks, as new details were slow to emerge, the coverage only got more embarrassing.

NBC went a full two hours on Wednesday, dropping its *World's Most Amazing Videos* at 9 p.m. and substituting a special episode of *Dateline* about the high school killings titled *The Day After*. ABC's 20/20 devoted its entire hour to the incident, and set the low point when ABC reporter Bill Ritter asked the parents of the only black student killed in the massacre, "At some time you're going to have to identify your child's body. How hard is that going to be?"

Classy move, Bill. Let the healing begin.

Even MGM Home Entertainment got into the healing when they attempted to recall all video copies of *The Basketball Diaries,* a movie that depicts a dream sequence in which Leonardo DiCaprio shoots a teacher and students while wearing a long, black trenchcoat. "We are going to attempt to get as many of these videos off the shelf as possible," a studio spokesman told Thursday's Wall Street Journal. "We think it's the responsible thing to do under the circumstances."

Now, that's thinking.

How about we pull *The Terminator* also? Didn't Arnie have a black trenchcoat in that one, too? Let's not forget *The Matrix*. In fact, why not get rid of every movie that ever depicted any act of sensationalized violence, in the event that somebody somewhere out there may copy it?

Get real.

In the last hundred years, over 160,000 films have been produced, examining the human condition from the most finite to the most sensationalized and trivialized. Tragedy occurs in every wake of live and under any circumstance, and while Hollywood is quick to make a buck from the image of Keanu Reeves wearing a trenchcoat, it doesn't mean that art must be watered down to it's most milquetoast to satisfy those always looking to point a finger.

A lot of good points have been made in the past week. Yes, I agree that *Jerry Springer* should air at night. Yes, I feel that communication with our children and an ongoing dialogue is paramount to avert the type of emotional crushing that leads to someone opening fire on classmates for making fun of them. Yes, I feel the media is partially responsible, but as a community, we're hypocritical.

Admit it, we're a nation of rubberneckers. How many times has traffic slowed to a stop because everybody has to see the guy on the side of the road changing his tire? That immediate gratification for the sensational spills over into our viewing habits. We watch reality TV like *Cops, Jerry Springer*, and Fox crap like *When Cars Attack*, but as soon as somebody decides to go postal, suddenly it's the bad, bad media that must be taken to task for its irresponsibility.

That's like a drug addict getting pissed at the dealer when somebody overdoses. Hey, the dealer's just providing what is requested, just as the revenue-hungry networks are pandering to what people want to see.

It's very simple. If nobody watches, it will go away. High-quality television shows are canceled all the time. Why? Because nobody's watching. If the entertainment industry is so bad, video games are so violent, and the whole shebang nothing more than a salad bar of bad ideas, then turn the television off and pick up a book. The truth is, as much as we'd like to blame movies, music or books, there's never going to be a clear-cut explanation for why people do what they do.

The true irony here is that just as Hollywood is recalling their own movies and the network news broadcast solemn-voiced town square meetings, somebody somewhere is already at a word processor plinking out *Terror In The Rockies: The Motion Picture.*

And I'll bet that when the TV-movie depicting the horrible events in Denver airs during sweeps week, it will be the most-watched television program in the nation.

The massacre at Columbine High School was one of those defining moments when the world united in the shock and horror as events unfolded on their TV's. The images made me think of family and friends, and the randomness of fate. I will never forget the fear I had for the kid who dangled from the library window, or how touched I was by the story of the teacher shot while directing students to safety, and who asked to see pictures of his family as he lay dying.

These flash moments of heroism and helplessness are there to remind us how precious life is, not to be packaged and sold.

Syriana: The Feel-Bad Movie of the Year

November 23, 2005

Syriana is an old-fashioned political intrigue tale in which the ideas barely spoken are scarier than anything presented on screen. It's only when asked his thoughts, that Bryan Woodman (Matt Damon), an oil price analyst, tells a conflicted prince what the film had thus far been only suggesting: that in the end, oil is a dwindling commodity, and whoever controls it will have all the power and money because the world does not know how else to operate.

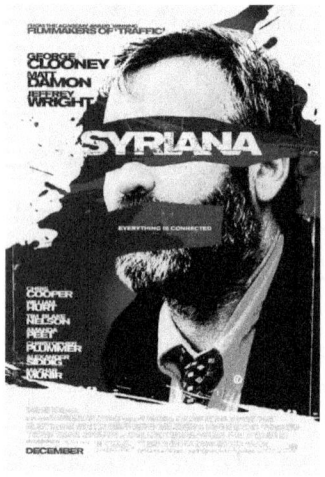

And while we are all down here calling each other names, the oil companies are posting obscene profits while gas prices skyrocket. The high price of gas is something everyone on either side of the political divide can relate to, which is why *Syriana* is maybe the most vital and time-specific American film since *The China Syndrome*.

Writer-director Stephen Gaghan won an Oscar for his twisty adaptation *Traffic*, which interwove stories to create a quilt work of stories. In *Syriana*, five or six stories unfold in what seems like uninterrupted cinema time. There are missing pieces, as if something was happening while you were channel surfing. The result is a film you have to pay attention to, but it's all there.

Bob Baer (George Clooney) is a burned out CIA operative who must have been a bad-ass at one time - there are glimpses of it - but he is now a frightened, overweight shell of himself coasting on contacts and old tricks. He is offered one last gig - to assassinate a prince who is the heir apparent to the throne, the same prince who has just granted natural gas drilling rights - long held by Connex, a Texas energy giant - to a higher Chinese bid.

Jimmy Pope (Chris Cooper) owns Killen, the smaller oil company that awaits the federal approval of a merger with Connex that would make it one of the largest in the world; Connex wants the smaller company's drilling rights in Kazakhstan. Bennett Holiday (Jeffrey Wright) is the Washington attorney in charge of guiding the Connex-Killen merger. He needs to give the Justice Department enough material to make their case against Killen for its shady dealings in Kazakhstan without jeopardizing the entire deal, which means at least one or two heads are going to roll. He has to choose which ones, which makes his very name ironic.

Seemingly unrelated, there are two Pakistani workers who lose their jobs because of the merger consolidation. They are embraced by a Muslim cleric who may convince them that martyrdom is a good thing.

And that's just the beginning. Every story is a satellite that crosses the orbit of every other story but contains its own world within. Each character has a personal demon or vice, an outside force that affects and shapes everything they do onscreen. Each character could be the main character of his (or her) own film.

That Gaghan manages to makes sense of all this is a minor miracle. There are several Big Moments that would be the centerpiece of any lesser film but unfold matter-of-factly and with grace here. In fact, for a film with such an epic scope, it's very easy to be caught off guard by the very human moments.

A boy dies in a swimming pool, a scene that is heart-wrenching. But then fifteen minutes later, his father is away on a business trip and passes time swimming. The juxtaposition itself is stirring; that the camera cranes high enough that the man appears as an ant in a blue puddle only illustrates the emotional core of this film: that no matter what these people do, they are all, in their own ways, alone.

Amanda Peet is a revelation as a grieving wife, and Damon simply has great taste when choosing his roles. Alexander Siddig is the optimistic Prince Nasir, who waits patiently for his father, the Emir, to choose which son will succeed him. Christopher Plummer, Chris Cooper and Jeffrey Wright are all solid, with the latter so knotted up, he looks like the "before" side of a Pepto Bismol ad.

The performances are superlative, none more so than Clooney, whose Bob Baer is a bloated failure of a man whose name inspires looks of sympathy from his colleagues. His eyes register two emotions at all times: weariness and desperation, as if he had forgotten a long time ago just what the hell he was doing all the way across the world. But underneath it all is a trained killing machine, and when he needs to threaten somebody, he doesn't have to raise his voice doing so.

But the tables do turn and after Clooney becomes the fall guy, he sets out to find out why and who set him up. There's also a nasty little torture scene that surpassed the toe smashing in Mel Gibson's *Payback* in terms of supreme "it could happen" gross-out moments.

It's Clooney's finest hour, and frankly the kind of performance that is so achingly real that it's more unpleasant to watch than the kind of showy turn that wins awards. You just feel bad for the poor bastard, and when things go wrong for him, I just didn't want to watch it happen.

It's worth noting that Clooney didn't just find this gig - his production company Section Eight (which he operates with director Steven Soderbergh) got the ball rolling and both Clooney and Soderbergh are executive producers.

Syriana is an outstanding, albeit long film, and never tries to be a crowd pleaser. Sure, Matt Damon and Clooney co-starred in the *Ocean's Eleven* movies but never once is there the slightest wink or forced moment between them, and that sheer absence of cinematic light might be too much for people simply wanting to be entertained. For those folks, I offer this: Clooney will make *Ocean's Thirteen* someday.

But for now - and on the heels of his own *Good Night and Good Luck* (which he co-wrote and directed) - there is no other actor in Hollywood using his movie star cache at this level. In 2005 alone, he has contributed two of the most prescient and unsettling glances behind the curtain at industries that both seem infallible and arrogant: the news media and the oil industry.

Remember Gordon Gekko's 80's mantra, "greed is good"? Tim Blake Nelson one-ups him in a brief, but destined to be classic exchange: "Corruption? Corruption is our protection. Corruption keeps us safe and warm. Corruption is why you and I are prancing around in here instead of fighting over scraps of meat out in the street. Corruption ... is why we win."

And yeah, that's sorta scary.

Michael Jackson: Human Nature Wins

October 31, 2009

NOTE: This was one of those cases where I went all-in with the best of intentions, to honor Michael Jackson's memory by taking a stand against exploiting him, but man, I was voted down! As cynical and obvious as this film was to me, I've never gotten as much "hate mail" as I did after posting the following review:

It's hard to separate the dazzling moments from the stench that permeates *Michael Jackson: This is It*, a hastily-assembled montage of Jackson's personal rehearsal footage for the series of concerts scrapped in the wake of the legendary singer's unexpected death on June 26, 2009.

It's electrifying to watch him operating even at half-capacity and a sobering reminder of a towering talent lost. It's also hard not to get caught up in Jackson's playful spirit. Yes, he was all business and is revealed to be involved in every aspect of the production, even directing those around him as he practiced himself.

But *This* is not a concert film because there was no concert. It's also not a full documentary because aside from an introduction card explaining where the footage came from and a quick-cut montage of Jackson's awkward press announcement to frame the footage, there is no sense of narrative, momentum, ebb and flow or purpose.

His death is never once mentioned so there is no cathartic finale, no global connection the way his televised funeral galvanized the world. This is more like what the bonus footage on the DVD would have looked like, except, well, there is no concert DVD.

Sure, the editing is crisp and fast-paced, but it also seems clunky and rushed, which it was.

Let's face it, Jackson never wanted this particular footage to be seen. He was a perfectionist and would be mortified to know images of him being thrown off by his bulky in-ear monitor were playing on 3,400 screens around the world. The only reason this film exists is because AEG, the company that invested tens of millions of dollars into Michael Jackson and his tour, wanted a return on their investment.

There is no reason why, if this film had to exist, that the powers-that-be couldn't have invested a little more time and care so that in twenty years, it was remembered as definitive, powerful work. It's not like they didn't have a powerful subject or story.

But as it stands, *This Is It* feels like a work-in-progress, a formless mass that may contain amazing images and sounds, but resonates only because of our collective response to those great songs, not because there was any care that went into this crass money-grab of a film.

At the beginning we see a card that says "For his fans" but it might have well have read "For his investors."

POSTSCRIPT:

I underestimated the deep appreciation people had for Jackson's work and that seeing this film was part of a cultural grieving process. I get that now. I still maintain it was a cash-grab, but in the end, none of that mattered to the fans. They wanted one last chance to see Jackson in the zone, and that's what they got, for better or worse.

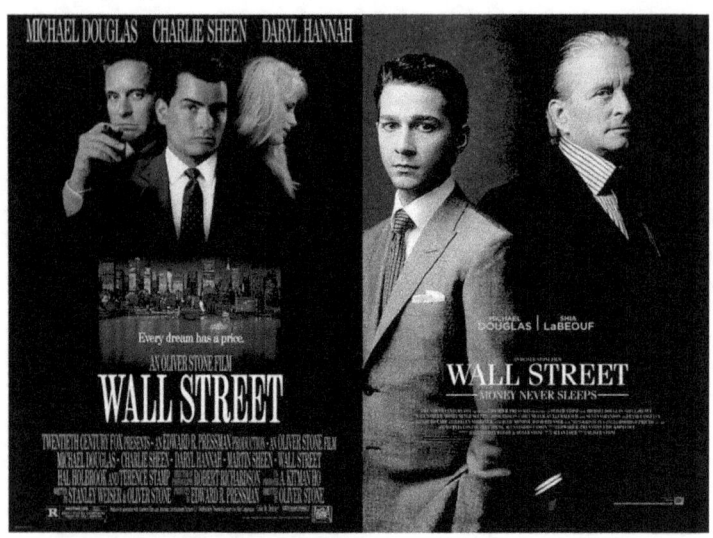

Wall Street: The Wrong Sequel at the Right Time

September 30, 2010

Oliver Stone's sequel to his iconic 1987 *Wall Street* arrives at just the right moment. Given the financial dire straits we find ourselves in and the spectacular bubble burst that led to banks disappearing overnight and government intervention, there has never been a more relevant time for the return of Gordon Gekko (Douglas, reprising his Oscar-winning role).

But instead of crafting another zeitgeist-defining film, Stone's sequel tries to be all things to all people: a cautionary tale about the evils of corruption; a clarion call about who's handling our precious financial futures; a touchy-feely character study about a reformed snake wanting to reconnect with his estranged daughter; a love story about two kids trying to make it in this crazy world with all that money flying around; and ultimately a sequel with crowd-pleasing call-outs to that previous flick.

Jake Moore (LaBeouf) and Winnie Gekko (Mulligan) are a cute couple, except for one small thing. She hates her famous white collar criminal father, now freed from prison, and wants nothing to do with him. Jake seeks out the legendary baron after his mentor's (Frank Langella) banking firm is destroyed by mega-tycoon Bretton James (Josh Brolin).

Jake wants revenge. Gekko wants a relationship with his daughter. The devil, as always, is in the details. Of course all of this family melodrama happens against the backdrop of the looming 2008 financial crisis, the same way that Jack and Rose happened on the Titanic. Screenwriting 101 tells us that the story serves the theme. Even though much is made of the catchphrase "Greed is Good" and the new buzzworthy meme "Moral Hazard," neither really applies because even after seeing the film, I'm still not sure what Oliver Stone is selling. Certainly all that retro-quirky David Byrne music is meant to evoke something but I'm not sure "1980s Bette Midler comedies" are what Stone had in mind.

Then there is the issue of the pacing and editing. Back in the day, Stone might have ruffled some feathers but you could always count on him for a blistering narrative with crisp, daring transitions and at least one white-hot lightning rod of a statement. Think *Natural Born Killers. JFK. Nixon.*

Wall Street: Money Never Sleeps doesn't even evoke the taut drama of the first film. Now every time someone launches into a story with a sad ending, the plinky synth piano kicks in to let us know it's time to feel bad.

And even though Stone has never been accused of subtlety, did we really need not one but two shots of big, luminous bubbles floating through the air, ready to pop?

Of course, the main attraction is Douglas, playing an older, wiser Gordon Gekko. Both the actor and character are grayer, more weathered, and nimble, as if either has nothing more to lose. When Gekko recounts the loss of his son to drugs, it's hard not to feel bad for Douglas. But this wouldn't be a *Wall Street* movie if Gordon Gekko was going out quietly as a feeble old man. It's only a matter of time until those claws come out.

And that's why it's a shame that when Gekko invokes a stunning betrayal that conveniently levels his enemies, Stone doesn't even allow us the satisfaction of watching it happen.

LaBeouf and Mulligan are attractive, capable actors but are only able to do so much opposite heavyweights like Douglas and Brolin. Maybe that's the point. They look out of place and that's probably by design. Mulligan is the de facto heart of the movie, even though she has a few secrets too.

Josh Brolin is arrogant and commanding, a perfect villain, who even makes the innocent line "You figured out a way to get my attention" sound scary. Brolin and Douglas bring oiliness and gravitas to every coiled exchange.

But movies like this are supremely frustrating. They have something to say and a fully-invested cast bringing heavyweight performances. The dialogue is crisp, the tasty character moments sublime. Charlie Sheen reprises his role as Bud Fox in a tasty cameo that's made all the more outrageous following his 2011 media flameout.

The first film was a bitter pill with a warning. This sequel is all about the empty calories. It's "ripped from the headlines" but it's not cathartic. It ends not with an ominous sense of dread but with the kind of ingenuous finale of a thousand romantic comedies.

This is the wake-up call Oliver Stone thinks we need?

4 A LONG TIME AGO...

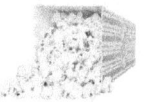

(...1999, TO BE EXACT)

"*Wars* not make one great." - Yoda
"No shit!" - Buford T. Justice

The following columns were written in the run-up to the release of *Star Wars, Episode I: The Phantom Menace,* and to say that the movie world and this humble reviewer were in the throes of *Star Wars* mania is an understatement.

It had been two years since the Special Edition re-releases of *Star Wars* (1977), *The Empire Strikes Back* (1980) and *Return of the Jedi* (1983) had conquered the box office, and there was little question that the new film would set records. No mere sequel, this was a project financed entirely by creator George Lucas that would push the limits of digital effects, going so far to promise photo-realistic CGI characters for the first time.

In hindsight, it's clear to see that fanboys and the larger film community was getting all lathered up for what *The Phantom Menace* could do in terms of changing the technical aspects of cinema, and likely challenging *Titanic* (1997) for the box office crown (*Star Wars* fans were still sore that James Cameron's blockbuster left the original film in its wake).

Nobody ever bothered to consider if the story would work or if the performances would be worth a damn, or how irritating Jar Jar Binks would be, or (the horror) what "midichlorians" are.

Try to spot the moment this humble reporter's expectations come crashing down to Earth ...

Pizza, Sex and Wing Commander

March 17, 1999

They say science-fiction is like pizza or sex. Even bad sci-fi is pretty good. I had a lot of time to think about that phrase while waiting for something to happen in *Wing Commander*, the latest in a failed line of video games that aspire to be feature film franchises.

The odd thing is that it's not like the evil Hollywood system got their dirty little hands on a sacred property and botched in. Nope, the director was none other than Chris Roberts, who created each of the wildly successful CD-ROM games. Changing the characters and spaceship designs are one thing.

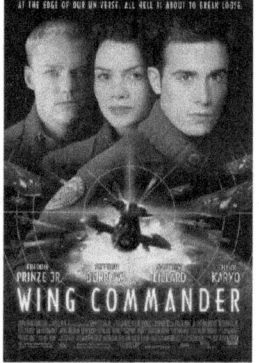

But *Wing Commander* fails in just about every cinematic category. First and foremost, the special effects - highly promoted as all digital - were dark and blurry. The spaceships, an important cornerstone to any cool sci-fi, were drab and boring. And the good guys' ship was called the Tiger Claw.

The Tiger Claw.

The writing is silly. To move from one non-event to the next, screenwriters Roberts and Kevin Droney filled as much space with techno-babble as they could, as well as an irritating combination of military terms like "bogey" with 25th century phrases like "Kilrathi."

Imagine a movie where people stand around looking at monitors, time out how long it will take the bad guys to reach Earth, argue, go out in blurry spaceships, go back in and look at some more monitors, argue, look at more monitors, argue some more...

Well, you get the picture.

The big finale has our heroes getting through the stargate first and picking off the bad guys as they come through. That's it. If someone could have just thought of this brilliant idea ten minutes in, I could have done something more important with my time.

Like, say, tie my shoes.

Ironically, on the very same day *Wing Commander* made its theatrical bow, so did the second trailer for *Star Wars, Episode I: The Phantom Menace*, and if it wasn't obvious to those who saw it on CNN or *Entertainment Tonight*, it rocked. There was more sheer cinema, more emotion, more plot, and more WOW in the two and a half minute trailer than in ten *Wing Commanders*.

I heard a couple of lunkheads complaining about *Phantom Menace* while waiting for Wing to start. You gotta love these guys, these cynical types who feel it's their job to stand up and share their opinions AT THIS VOLUME, and who always try to sound cool by dissing anything that's part of the mainstream. But bless them, the projectionist couldn't start *Wing Commander* fast enough for them.

There are those who will try valiantly to not get swept up in the hype, but they will ultimately fail. Let me say this now: In the same way that his early *Star Wars* films ushered in THX sound and unparalleled special effects, *The Phantom Menace* will change the playing field as we know it.

In addition, the next two *Star Wars* films will be created digitally - without any film - a development that may shock the cinephiles, but I'm sure putting sound in a movie was once a pretty crazy idea as well. It makes sense that Lucas wouldn't just create a new *Star Wars* film, but the tools in which to play it. He's premiering a new THX format with rear channel sound, a new digital projection system, and a movie to show with these new toys. The arrival of a new *Star Wars* movie isn't just more fodder for geeks. It's the beginning of a new way of movie-going.

So, the arrival of a 150-second trailer is, in fact, newsworthy. It's not studio-created hype to sell a crappy product. It's not a desperate attempt to recoup an investment. It's truly the beginning of a new millennium.

Phantom cost all of $110 million. That's less than half of what *Titanic* cost, and Lucas footed the entire bill. With *Phantom* now arriving two days earlier, on May 19th, that's an additional $20 million in the bank. Despite Lucas' insistence that he's not looking to set any box office records, he'd better get used to it.

I'm going to predict a five day sprint to $100 million, and a serious challenge to James Cameron's king of the world claim (*Titanic* made $600 million domestically and $1.8 billion around the world). *Phantom Menace* may not have the legs of *Titanic*, but it will make more money faster. It also has a more rabid fan base that could make up for the love story and Celine Dion aspect of the Cameron juggernaut.

It's gonna be one hell of a race.

Back to that pizza and sex analogy. If all sci-fi were like *Wing Commander*, I'd become a chaste vegetarian. Fortunately, every now and then, there's a *Star Wars* to expand the horizons and keep things interesting.

POSTSCRIPT:

See? Nowhere did I even *consider* the story would have absolutely no inertia or internal logic. I was salivating over all the toys. I was right on the money about *Episode I* hitting $100 million in five days, but the movie never came close to *Titanic*. It did ultimately pass the original *Star Wars* on the all-time list and through re-releases, scored a cool billion dollars at the box office.

Warning: Spoilers!

May 5, 1999

In 1983, when I was in high school, a guy in art class was babbling about how he had a bootleg copy of *Revenge On The Jedi* two months before it would be released. I'd been privy to bootlegged *Star Wars* before, so it was believable.

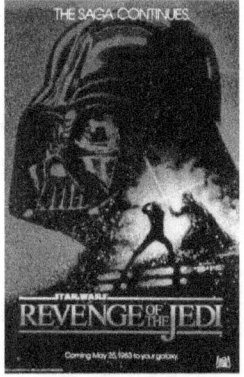

But stupid me, I asked him to prove it, and he said, "Well, Darth Vader really is Luke's father, Yoda dies, Princess Leia is Luke's sister..."

Whoa, whoa, WHOA!

I stopped him right there. He was spouting crazy talk, but there was a casualness about him that was disarming. Damned if two months later it didn't turn out to be true.

A year later, I was watching *Ghostbusters* for the first time, and toward the end, a kid said to his friend something like, "Here comes the marshmallow man." Before I could ponder the meaning of what he was talking about, Mr. Stay Puft lumbered onto the screen and the theaters erupted in laughter.

I wanted to pour my soda over the kid's head.

You hear it all the time. People recommend movies to their friends, and as opposed to letting them just watch the thing, they feel compelled to tell them who the killer really was, or what main character suddenly dies.

What's the point of ruining the ride for someone else? As someone who reports on film productions, information is my secret weapon. But as a lover of cinema--no, I DON'T particularly want to know who Anakin Skywalker's father is before I see *The Phantom Menace*. But there are scores of websites that will tell me if I do.

Promotion is the most integral part of a film's launch, yet so many studios give away the goods in the two minute trailer. I knew that the bus in *Speed* would explode because I saw it in the trailer, thereby placing that image in my head and making me wait the entire film for it.

Would *The Usual Suspects* be nearly as effective if we knew the secret of Keyser Sozé in advance? How about Faye Dunaway's family secret in *Chinatown*, or the identity of Rosebud in *Citizen Kane*? People were fairly respectful of the big secret in *The Crying Game*, but then Roger Ebert comes along and gives it away on his TV show. Thanks, Rog.

I liked *The Devil's Advocate*, but I suspect I would have liked it a hell of a lot more (pardon the pun), had Warner Bros. not told me in advance that Al Pacino's really the devil, something the movie does not tell us until the end.

Thus far, *Go* is my favorite film of 1999. But the press notes issued by Columbia Pictures to the reviewing media give away many of the surprises. After I saw the movie, I was thankful I didn't read the notes first. What a shame it would have been to know some of the real identities and situations before they happened.

Think I'm excluding the reviewers? They're the worst of the lot. We can shut our friends up, but we can't govern what the thumb and hat set are going to say.

Granted, it's not easy to review a film without giving away the twists and turns, but that doesn't stop some film critics from describing every last detail of a film so that audiences know the whole works going in.

Hey, just because some jaundiced tight-ass doesn't like their job anymore or is steamed because they're stuck reviewing movies as opposed to making them, doesn't mean they have to ruin it for the rest of us.

Yeah, I review movies, too. But I'm not gonna tell you the end before you see it. A friend recently asked me to tell her what happens at the end of a thriller she was going to rent, and I refused. She asked me repeatedly to tell her the end, so I told her something different. Sneaky? Sure, but she was as surprised as she should have been when the killer was revealed. She loved the movie, and didn't even remember I lied to her.

Star Wars, Episode I: The Phantom Menace opens in two weeks. I can wait two more weeks. I'm not gonna read the novel, the comic books, or even the toy packaging. I want the film to unfold for me the way it was designed to.

I will admit that youth played a part in the excitement of experiencing *Star Wars* the first time around. But after having seen thousands of movies, there's still nothing like the thrill of the cinema catching you off guard and taking you someplace completely unexpected.

You can find out all the surprises if you'd like, but as far as I'm concerned, my official policy until May 19th, is don't ask, don't tell.

The Phantom Menace: It's Finally Here!
May 19, 1999

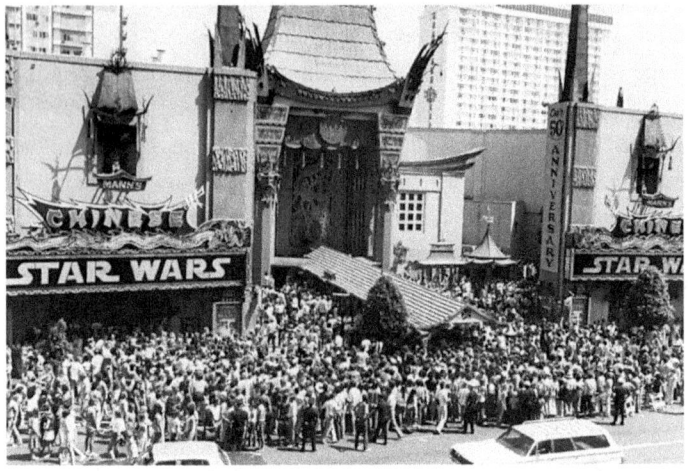

Picture if you will: you're a ten year old kid in 1977 when *Star Wars* is released. Forever, your world is changed.

You become interested in storytelling, and as technology evolves, you come to realize that nothing can be imagined anymore that can't be created and put up on a movie screen. It's only years later that you realize exactly what an important moment in your life it was when that galaxy far, far away was introduced to you.

Now, as the debut of the *Star Wars, Episode I: The Phantom Menace* nudges the entertainment industry into a filmless world with new sound systems, digital projection and entire characters that are computer generated, the Jedi prepare to face their most worthy adversaries: movie critics.

Welcome to my world.

Do I begin with the nostalgia I felt just two years ago when the original trilogy was re-released? Do I compare *The Phantom Menace* to other 90's movies? Do I shed all that baggage or haul it into the theater with me?

Such questions were soon put aside once the movie started. It sure looked and sounded like *Star Wars*, all right, with awesome FX, whooshing spaceships and that great, sweeping John Williams score. But it was immediately more ... vague?

We're plunged into a complicated political struggle within the Galactic Trade Federation, and the strings being pulled by said phantom menace, a certain Darth Sideous.

Although the early scenes unfold leisurely, the plot gets choppy toward the middle. Lucas is in no hurry to speed through the proceedings. In fact, much as *Return Of The Jedi* was a two hour climax, it appears that *The Phantom Menace* will be looked upon as a two-hour opening act. There are many new characters and species to introduce, and despite the slower-than-expected pace, no effort is made to stop the movie for such introductions. I guess that's what repeat viewings are for.

Plot specifics are best discovered by watching the film, but I'll say this much: The ground battle sequences are dynamic and the best of the series thus far. The final conflict, which takes place in three different locales simultaneously, is well-paced and dramatic. Lucas apparently was concerned that this elongated sequence might be confusing. It isn't.

As well, Darth Maul (the guy with the red and black face makeup and the dual lightsaber) is one bad ass dude. Unfortunately, his key line in the film, widely seen in the music video and trailer, goes unanswered (for now, at least), and his appearance, however dynamic, is all too brief.

The standout sequence is the pod race, a competition of illegal ship racing through the twisty desert canyons of Tatooine. If it was possible to construct a more suspenseful and dizzying sequence than the speeder bike scene in *Return Of The Jedi*, Lucas has done it here.

The performances are as solid as they can be, considering that Lucas notoriously uses humans the way he uses special effects. Natalie Portman is a bit wooden as the teen queen Padme/Amidala and I'm not sure if that's on purpose. Liam Neeson's Qui-Gon Ginn is an instant classic addition to the mythos, and I personally can't wait to see Samuel L. Jackson's Mace Windu pick up a lightsaber in future editions. Despite Jake Lloyd's early branding as "Mannequin Skywalker," he is far more satisfying in a kid role than you'd expect.

But it's hard not to feel a little deflated after the first viewing. After all, how can any mortal film live up to expectations like this? And maybe it's me, but everything and everyone seems a little too proper, a little too stiff. I still have fond memories of the original *Star Wars*, a movie in which every character yelled at each other. Again, I'm willing to give Lucas the benefit of the doubt that things will loosen up as the events grow more tense.

I could also pick a few nits about the relative lack of narrative momentum. Big Things happen but almost as if they have to that way. The best theory here is to place *Episode I* exactly where it belongs: at the beginning. It's the first episode, so therefore, there is a lot to introduce.

If anything, this installment acts as a glorious set-up to romance, betrayal and horrors that follow. George Lucas predicted that *Episode III* will probably make half the money of any of the others, because, by its very nature, it's the most dour.

This can only be good.

But for now, I cannot wait to see it again.

Star Wars: Over And Out

August 18, 1999

Too many media outlets have already done this one to death. But, I figured that since the summer's winding down, and the arrival of *Episode I* is now a good solid three months behind us, now would be the time to examine what worked, what didn't, and what George Lucas' Achilles Heel has been revealed to be.

The general consensus has been that *Star Wars, Episode I: The Phantom Menace* was not groundbreaking like the original, not character-driven like *The Empire Strikes Back*, but better overall than *Return Of The Jedi*. The box office has reflected this. *Episode I* has earned almost $420 million of this writing, a number that firmly places it on the All-Time list at No. 3 (behind *Titanic* and the original *Star Wars*).

Purists who embraced the mythology of the saga were disappointed by the slapstick antics, while others embraced the hate before actually seeing it. One guy was flummoxed to learn I kind of liked it, and went on for a good minute about how childish, how little plot, etc., until finally admitting he hadn't seen it yet.

The era of the armchair critic is upon us.

The merchandising and media hype - God, I hate that word - was inevitable. But even PepsiCo admitted that their *Defeat the Dark Side* contest triad (with Taco Bell, Kentucky Fried Chicken and Pizza Hut) failed miserably. Whoever had the brilliant idea of putting KFC's Colonel and the Taco Bell dog up against Battle Droids is probably *working* at a KFC now.

So, what did we learn? First, that *Episode I* was just a movie and not the Second Coming. and that *Star Wars* movies are mostly critic-proof. "Hype" can only do so much, certainly not $400 million.

And sadly, that King George is fallible.

Sure, he took digital film presentation into the next century, but the average moviegoer doesn't care about that.

They only care that Jar Jar is back on screen getting in the way of a perfectly good *Star Wars* movie, and, um, can he die soon? Please? Never in the *Star Wars* universe has a character inspired such wrath. There was even a website called jarjarmustdie.com.

Jar Jar was only slightly irritating to me but I can relate to the impassioned cries for his rabbit-eared head. I felt the same way about Chris Tucker in *The Fifth Element*.

Lucas spent much of his media time on how over 95% of the film was rendered within the computer. But he really should listen to some of the folks who think a good story beats effects every day of the week.

A few questions linger: How come Jedi Master Qui-Gon didn't disappear? How come the Jedis can't sense that Senator Palpatine - who's really Darth Sideous and who will become the Emperor - has that dark side of the Force mojo working overtime? Even Yoda didn't catch it. How about Threepio's memory loss? Lucas has told us that all will be explained.

The legacy of *Star Wars* has been dealt a blow. If the next two movies are more of the same - cutesy shtick, and characters taking a back seat to the FX - then the double trilogy will have just two movies, *Star Wars* and *The Empire Strikes Back*, which will be considered the good ones.

If the next two are really good, *Phantom Menace* will take its place as the *Godfather Part III* of the series - necessary in the grand scheme of things, but not the first one people reach for when heading to the video library.

As Yoda might say, "Uncertain, the future is."

A Disturbance In The Force

March 29, 2000

Man, George Lucas sure knows how to test the limits of his fan base. Since its May 1999 release, *Star Wars, Episode I: The Phantom Menace* has become the second biggest worldwide smash of all time with $922 million ($433m in the US alone), and smashed almost every speed record imaginable on the way to those totals.

You can only imagine how much *Episode I* would have made if it were actually good.

In the months following the cooling of the *Star Wars* machine, true dissention has set in. With little news to report, the fandom websites have latched onto another *Wars*-related topic that's hotter than a Tatooine summer.

Next week, Fox will release the film on VHS with no DVD in

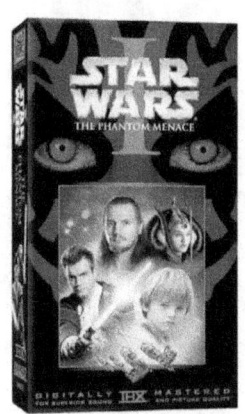

sight. The reaction was unanimous disillusionment, followed by a flurry of rumors suggesting King George may after all, have a DVD surprise for us. Alas, starwars.com shortly thereafter, released the following official statement:

"There is no plan to release any of the *Star Wars* films on DVD for the foreseeable future and definitely not this year. George Lucas would like to do something special with the DVD release. Unfortunately he does not have time to concentrate on the DVD project at this time. George is currently working on the script for *Episode II* and preparing for principal photography that will begin this summer in Australia. The films will definitely be released on DVD. It's just that we don't know when."

So, let's break this down. George Lucas pushes the limits of technology to tell his story, creates a newly-enhanced THX sound system, and then insists that only theaters equipped with the new sound will be allowed to show the film, thereby guaranteeing the best possible presentation. But for the home release, we're stuck with clunky, fuzzy videotape.

This line of thinking probably came from the same part of the brain that thought Jar Jar Binks was a good idea.

I have a question. If Lucas is spending his precious time writing *Episode II*, then why doesn't he trust some of his most valued employees to oversee the *Phantom Menace* DVD transfer?

Heck, there's no need to even bother with the extras. Fans would be happy with a no-frills DVD transfer until whatever time he decides to release his special set, most likely a box of all six films. And those fans, I'm sure, would spring for both.

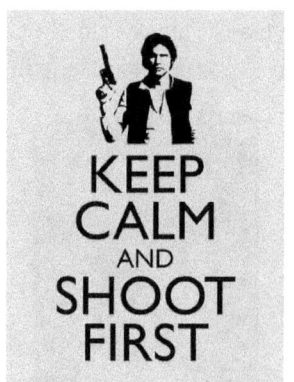

Could it be that George is planning to tinker with *Episode I* the way he did *IV*, *V* and *VI*? That would be the natural assumption, considering that he's never been one to actually *finish* a project and walk away from it.

In 1997, he gave us the re-mastered *Star Wars* trilogy, complete with shiny new effects and a handful of touches worth debating as to whether they actually helped or not. The digital backgrounds, yes. The re-dubbed Darth Vader dialogue at the end of *Empire* ... um, not really.

In fact, it can be argued that most of the time Lucas revisits one of his classics, he only diminishes the power of the work. Han Solo now shoots Greedo in defense, an act that weakens the character. A few frames missing from the Death Star prison break now erase the image of stormtroopers taking direct hits; and the aforementioned Darth Vader line "Bring my shuttle!" is replaced with casual dialogue about preparing his trip to the Star Destroyer.

But it's not just the *Star Wars* films. He also digitally altered the opening title sequence of *American Graffiti* when it was released in 1998, and re-titled (!) the classic 1981 Indy flick to *Indiana Jones and the Raiders of The Lost Ark*. Really rolls off the tongue, there, doesn't it? While he's at it, I'm sure there are a few parts of *Howard the Duck* that can also use some touching up.

I wouldn't be surprised if Lucas fiddles with his Skywalker saga some more before committing them to DVD. One can only imagine how he might alter *The Phantom Menace*. Some suggestions: Put back in that cool Darth Maul monologue about fear that played only in the commercials; Synch up the trade federation conspirators' words to match their three-pronged mouths a little better; and while you're at it, please, oh please, lose Jar Jar.

Star Wars has affected so many people so profoundly and inspired so many of today's filmmakers, that for George to pretend the saga is anything less would be remiss. Yes, we expect the best, because Lucas has trained us to. For him to skimp on quality or shortchange the narrative because he doesn't really enjoy writing is nothing short of a betrayal.

It was the fans that escalated his films to legend, and the fans that responded so favorably to Timothy Zahn's early 90's novels that started the whole thing rolling again.

And in exchange for the $922 million the fans spent to support a film they felt less than enthusiastic about, they simply want one thing: a copy of *The Phantom Menace* on DVD.

I don't think it's too much to ask for.

Send In The Clones

August 15, 2001

There, now I can say I was the first to use that title because every half-witted critic in the land will surely follow suit next May.

I'm of course, referring to George Lucas' decision to call the next installment in the *Star Wars* series *Episode II: Attack Of The Clones*. Funny, I had the same reaction to *The Phantom Menace* the first time I heard that one. I thought it was a joke, until I went to starwars.com and had it confirmed for me.

The reaction wasn't pretty. Ewan McGregor -- Obi-Wan Kenobi himself -- called it a "terrible, terrible title." Employees of Pixar Animation began posting alternative titles that included: *Attack of the Killer Clones, Killer Clones from Outer Space* and *Dude, Where's My Clone?* The British entertainment website Popcorn.com carried word of the title, and then commented: Stop laughing, we're serious.

To understand Lucas' propensity for kitschy monikers, I suppose the signs point to his love of the old *Flash Gordon* movie serials, which began in 1936. I happen to love those serials too, despite chapters with titles like *The Planet Of Peril, Shattering Doom*

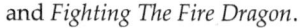

and *Fighting The Fire Dragon*.

Upon some digging, I realized they're also riffs on episodes from Lucas' *Young Indiana Jones* series: *The Phantom Train of Doom* and *Attack of the Hawkmen*. The literal approach is more straight-forward than the faux-intellect approach that many hipster filmmakers prefer today. *Attack Of The Clones* is an old-fashioned title that could be designed to appeal to lovers of adventure.

Of course, it's also time to get that ball rolling again and having a name for a movie that's been called *Episode II* for two years isn't a bad thing. It brings us one step closer and turns the pre-hype machine up a notch.

Last time this happened, with *Episode I: The Phantom Menace*, I purposefully avoided all the internet spoilers, even passing up an opportunity to read the script three weeks before it opened. But I had to realize a few key points that I may have overlooked before:

First, I'm not twelve anymore. Second, the movie wasn't all that great. Sure, it was *Star Wars*: It had the opening scroll, the great John Williams moments, great effects, and a handful of sequences that were pure magic: the final lightsaber duel, the podrace, the-- um, well that was about it. But I realized after that first viewing that I'd insulated myself for no reason.

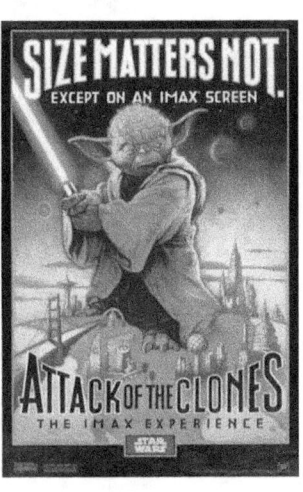

The Phantom Menace wasn't *Episode I* so much as it was a preface. It had very little, if nothing to do with the bigger part of the story, and was simply a series of meetings. Yeah, it was nice seeing nobody realize who the Emperor was, but it just wasn't enough. If it was, fans wouldn't have cut their own version and called it *The Phantom Edit,* losing almost 20 minutes and most of Jar-Jar's scenes.

So this time, I decided no spoiler or internet coverage was so shocking that I'd avert my eyes. I was raised on *Star Wars* and dammit, I want to enjoy it. If that means I uncover a whopper like "I am your father," then so be it, Jedi. As long as the possibility exists that *Episode II* will be as sucky as the first, then at least I want to enjoy it all now.

But from what I've read, it doesn't sound sucky at all. Theforce.net had a scriptment that took all the hearsay, smuggled reports and documented sequences and builds a complete look at the *Episode II* storyline and nuances.

I gotta tell you, the night I put my feet up and read this spoiler-laden summary was the most *Star Wars* fun I've had since seeing the Special Editions on the big screen with a hyped crowd.

But before you go looking for it, the website explains "The scriptment has been removed at the request of LucasFilm. We're sorry if you've come looking for it. Be sure to search our archives for older reports. If you're net savvy, you can find it, and it's a cracking good read. I'm hoping that the movie will be half as exciting."

But about that title: The official spin from LucasFilm is that the name "harkens back to the sense of pure fun, imagination and excitement that characterized the classic movie serials and pulp space fantasy adventures that inspired the *Star Wars* saga."

Did people react the same way in 1979 when we learned the long-awaited follow up was called *The Empire Strikes Back*? I remember not liking it, but I got over it quickly. Hey, I was twelve and the movie was so damn good, it earned the right to be called whatever it wanted.

Are we more cynical now? Definitely. Do we expect too much from the hype? Absolutely. Is it possible *Episode II* will be good enough to make us forget about the fact that *Attack Of the Clones* sounds pretty goofy?

I'm hoping so. But in many ways, I just wish I was twelve again.

Episode III: The Circle is Now Complete

May 19, 2005

In anticipation of *Star Wars, Episode III: Revenge Of The Sith*, I watched *Episode I* and *II* back-to-back. Having not seen either in some time, I was struck by how our memories tend to play tricks on us, especially regarding a property so hotly contested as George Lucas' tale set a long time ago in a galaxy far, far away.

As pop culture and netizens have dictated, the first two episodes sucked. For my money, I enjoyed *Episode II* quite a bit, especially the parts that didn't contain the love story.

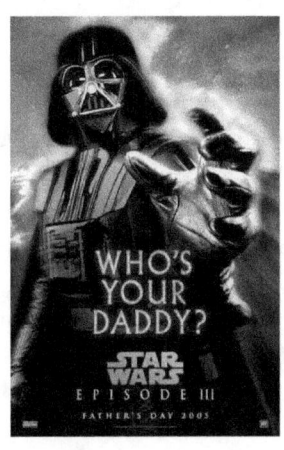

It has been very difficult for people who grew up geeking out on *Star Wars* in 1977 to accept the choices Lucas has made: from Anakin Skywalker's cherub-faced 10-year-old in *Episode I,* to the seemingly endless boardroom politics, to the infamous Jar Jar. Seeing those movies again, I bristled at a few things I'd forgotten about, but not because George - *how dare he?* - had a vision of what his *Star Wars* story was to be.

The sweeping tale of political subversion and personal salvation is certainly ambitious, and when the dust settles, there will be one story comprised of six chapters that tell the rise, fall and redemption of Anakin Skywalker. Declaring the prequel trilogy dead because of Jar Jar always seemed a little too easy.

Lucas certainly had a lot to achieve with *Episode III*. Officially, it needed to bridge the trilogies, pay everything off the first two prequels set up and connect all the dots in a compelling way. Oh, and unofficially, it couldn't "suck."

So let me report by saying that *Revenge Of The Sith* is probably as good as it could have been. If *Episodes I* and *II* lowered my expectations, *Episode III* sucker punched me in a good way.

Concluding the story of how Anakin Skywalker (Hayden Christensen) turns into Darth Vader, Lucas surprises by making every scene have an urgency that builds to a tragic climax. Yes, we all know what happens, but we don't know how and that's precisely what George got to play with as a writer and director. It also didn't hurt that he allegedly had playwright Tom Stoppard and Carrie Fisher clean up some of the dialogue.

Opening with a dizzying and swooping entry into a space battle in progress, we follow Obi-Wan Kenobi (Ewan McGregor) and Anakin Skywalker (Hayden Christensen) as they bravely set out to rescue Senator Palpatine (Ian McDiarmid), who has been kidnapped by separatist leader Count Dooku (Christopher Lee). The entire scenario ultimately exists to push Anakin into a merciless act that has the tragic result of pushing over the first Dark Side domino. Once the scene concludes, Palpatine knows that Anakin is, pardon the phrase, palpable.

And begun, the conversion has.

McDiarmid brings classic Shakespearian oiliness to the table as he dangles stories of Sith warlords with the power to heal and plays upon Anakin's insecurities and frustrations. A scene in an exclusive box at an opera is all dialogue, but creates more tension and sparks than most lightsaber battles.

The key line in the opening title crawl is "There are enemies on both sides." Anakin's arrogance allows him to be manipulated by the Republic and it's malevolent Sith lord Palpatine; and the future rebels, the separatists, who were once seen as the troublesome extremists but are now starting to sound like they make some sense

(I couldn't help but notice the rather analogous comparison to our own troubled planet and leaders who promise peace but steer us into war).

Palpatine convinces Anakin that the Jedis are the ones hell bent on taking control, playing into the young man's paranoia and forcing him to choose some absolutes. If the Jedi are to be dealt with, that means killing his friend and mentor, Obi-Wan, as well. Christensen plays these moments well.

Naively, he has come to believe that turning to the dark side will allow him to save wife Padme (Natalie Portman), who, his prescient dreams tell us, will die during childbirth. Anakin's good intentions truly pave his road to hell - or the burning lava world of Mustafar that will see master and apprentice face off in the ultimate example of agreeing to disagree.

The Duel, as it's been referred to, is angry and tragic, with a minimum of wasted chatter. The classic exchange prior to first blow says it all. The fates are in motion and the final choices of both these characters play into their six-film arc beautifully.

Once "Order 66" is given and the clone army turns on the Jedis, the film begins a steady and operatic march toward inevitability. Death is everywhere, and to Lucas' credit, he doesn't take the cute way out this time. Heads and limbs roll. Women and children are slaughtered. Beloved characters are wiped out.

I've often said that Lucas would have made a great silent film director, but in this case, it's particularly relevant. Because of the brevity of the script, the actors actually get to *act* this time around.

Unlike the first two movies in which good actors rush from line to line, here there is some gravitas, soul searching, and the general feeling that these people are coming up with these lines and choices themselves. For Lucas, this is a huge accomplishment as *Episode III* features some of the best acting in the entire series.

Despite some 30 pounds of muscular bulk, Hayden Christensen still comes off sort of as slight but he broods effectively well. His scenes with Natalie Portman flow more naturally, although she somehow becomes the weak acting link this time. Ewan McGregor owns the Obi-Wan role and brings subtle shadings to the second half of the film. The worse things get, the more he wears it on his face and by the finale, this guy looks like he's been completely beaten down.

Finally, Ian McDiarmid is the stand-out, infusing his Machiavellian Palpatine with the seasoned grace of a puppet master before evolving into his true bug-eyed villainous self. It is one of the great performances in Sci-fi history, equally hammy and frightening.

While we're talking about acting, it should be noted that Yoda's digital performance is so flawless, there is never a question that he lives onscreen with the rest of the cast. When bad things start to go down and he slumps over because his little green heart is breaking, so does ours. If there is an argument for a digital creation to replace an old-school puppet, this is it.

It's not a perfect film, but many of the problems stem from Lucas' earlier choices in setting up this chapter. And it might have been nice to leave one or two questions unanswered. You mean to tell me C-3PO and R2D2 are going to hang out on the same ship for 20 years until the events that open *Star Wars*?

And that Obi-Wan, while hiding out as a "crazy old hermit" on Tatooine would still wear his old Jedi robes but barely recall a time when he was called "Obi-Wan?" Note to Lucas: you couldn't think of any other Jedi uniform *other* than Alec Guinness' shabby old robes?

Despite itself, *Revenge of the Sith* succeeds as a rousing and sobering entry in the Star Wars canon.

The circle is now complete, thank the maker.

5 STRANGE NEW WORLDS

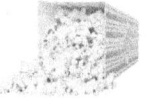

...OR HOW TO RUIN A GOOD THING.

As if it wasn't obvious before, I was a *Star Wars* kid. But it wasn't just that galaxy far, far away that inspired my imagination.

Long before *Star Wars*, I grew up watching reruns of *Star Trek* in syndication, as well the *Flash* Gordon movie serials, *Buck* Rogers, *Logan's Run*, *Planet of the Apes*, *Space: 1999* and *The Incredible Hulk*.

Science-fiction is the one genre with the ability to illuminate and comment on history and culture, and create progressive answers to unasked questions. And while remaining objective is the greatest challenge of every film critic, mine is finding the sweet spot between my jaded worldview and my inner child. Mainly because my inner child still thinks spaceships and ray guns are cool.

Needless to say, I find myself writing about sci-fi properties a lot, mainly because I can't understand why - even though they are the easiest way to build a lasting franchise - they always seem to be cut off at the knees by the powers that be.

Sci-fi is not only lucrative but, when done right, creates a lasting bond. There is no greater love than that between fanboys (and fangirls) and the object of their affection.

Think I'm kidding?

Go to any pop culture convention like WonderCon or Comic Con and you will find the presence of the Browncoats, a collective dedicated to the resurrection of Joss Whedon's beloved series *Firefly* - a show that lasted all of 14 weeks.

James Cameron: King of the Universe

December 20, 2009

We've seen it all before. But, we really haven't. Not this way.

The story of a man who enters a foreign culture only to realize he's been living the wrong life is as old as cave paintings. In particular, the story of a military man who realizes his very enemy

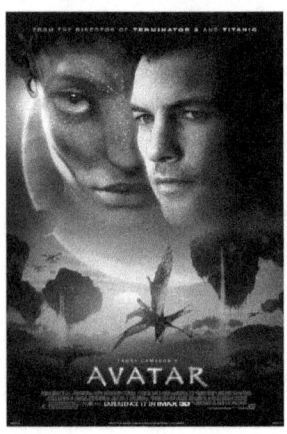

is a soulful and persecuted people, inspiring him to turn on his own kind, reached a cultural apex with Best Picture winner *Dances with Wolves*. But there was also *Battle for Terra* earlier this year, which had the exact same Sci-fi take on the story as *Avatar*.

In making the story about militaristic humans and the Na'vi, the 12-foot tall indigenous blue-toned inhabitants (with strong Native American overtones) of the alien planet Pandora, writer-director James Cameron didn't change a single beat of that story, and why should he? It's primal and it works.

Sam Worthington plays paralyzed ex-Marine Jake Sully, a genetic match for a deceased brother who was taking part in the science arm of a military occupation (Humans have landed on lush forest moon Pandora with massive mining gear and enough firepower to make Jesus weep in search of a rare pricey mineral cheekily named Unobtanium).

Jake will inhabit a chamber and awaken in a biologically-engineered alien Na'vi body (avatar) so he can interact and learn everything about them. Scientists seek to better understand the pagan-like race that can plug into its planet like a laptop to a network. But the military and corporate goons have other ideas.

If you've seen *Dances with Wolves*, I don't need to draw you a map as to where Jake's allegiances will ultimately lie so I'll spare the details here. But on his way to realizing the Evil That (Human) Men Do, we learn about the Na'vi and see things we've never seen on a movie screen before. That's not to say we haven't seen similar floating mountains and winged creatures on Roger Dean album covers, but that's another subject.

His films have always featured strong women but Neytiri is a fierce goddess, a combination of earthy, lethal and sexy. There is a moment after she saves Jake by killing a nasty beast, that she admonishes him for making her do it. It's one hell of an introduction.

With *Avatar*, James Cameron puts it all on the table and rolls some pretty big dice. But anyone caught up in the hype wasn't around or paying attention in the lead-up to *Titanic*. Nothing about the ocean liner epic was a done deal. Its budget was too high, they said. People know the ending, Blah blah blah. What *Titanic* truly had going for it wasn't just Leo and that Celine Dion song.

Titanic had James Cameron, and that's the difference.

Cameron is the classically-uppity auteur determined to make movies his way, dammit. His just happen to cost $250 million. But he's also no less than this century's Cecil B. DeMille, delivering envelope-pushing crowd-pleasing spectacle every damn time. George Lucas must hate his guts.

Cameron's vision of the planet Pandora, with its vast waterfalls, savage beasts and living neural network of soulful trees is simply stunning. My head knows that it's all computer wizardry but that never mattered any time the beautiful Neytiri (Zoe Saldana) lets out a guttural wail to show her heart is breaking.

Cameron is no less than this century's Cecil B. DeMille, delivering crowd-pleasing spectacle every damn time. Say what you will about the man's dialogue (and people have), he doesn't skimp on the visuals. Technically speaking, *Avatar* features the most effective use of 3D I've ever seen, never egregiously violating the fourth wall but using its dimensions to create an immersive environment. Cameron has created a masterpiece filled with strong performances, mythic arcs, exotic creatures and unforgettable visuals that will invariably change the way films are made.

Avatar may wear its influences like bumper stickers but there is no denying it's a rock 'em, sock 'em crowd pleaser greater than the sum of its parts. King of the world? Try King of the Universe

POSTSCRIPT:

Cameron did it again, with *Avatar* besting his own *Titanic* to become the biggest modern blockbuster of all time with over $2.7 billion at the global box office. However, it won just three of its nine Oscar nominations, losing Best Picture and Director to Cameron's ex-wife Kathryn Bigelow and her war flick *The Hurt Locker*.

Can Star Trek Live Long and Prosper?

July 7, 1999

We've spent so much time concentrating on that galaxy far, far away, that while nobody was looking, things in the 23rd century have taken a turn for the worst. The future ain't what it used to be.

Granted, *Star Trek* has been through a lot. In the 1960s, NBC bounced it all over the dial for three years, finally canceling Gene Roddenberry's beleaguered wagon train to the stars two years before their initial five year mission was completed. The rest is Hollywood history.

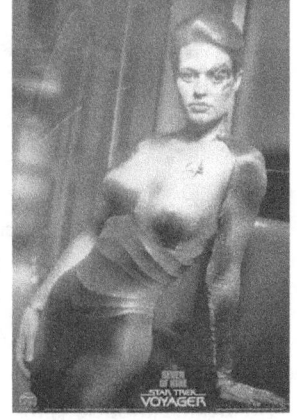

Star Trek became the tube's first major syndicated smash, spawning a cartoon series, nine big screen movies and three different spin-off series. In all, over 450 hours of *Star Trek* have come from Roddenberry's original vision.

Lately though, the Starship Enterprise has been rocked by forces more powerful than the Borg Queen experiencing PMS.

Deep Space Nine recently wrapped it's seventh year with no plans to follow Captain Picard and his *Next Generation* pals to the big screen; *Star Trek: Voyager* resorted to adding a voluptuous Borg babe to juice up it's flaccid ratings, and to boot, the ninth feature, *Star Trek: Insurrection* made $71 million, just a notch over what it cost to make.

Add to the mix the recent death of the beloved DeForest Kelley, who portrayed Dr. McCoy on the original series and in six films, and you've got a future suffering the blues.

Last week, Viacom honcho Jonathan Dolgen declared that the *Star Trek* franchise has to be re-imagined and made cheaper, in obvious reference to the rampant salary hikes that helped make *Insurrection* the most expensive and least profitable *Trek* thus far.

More disturbing is this little piece of news from Starfleet: Brannon Braga and Rick Berman are writing a two-hour pilot script which is said to have working title of *Star Trek: Flight Academy* and is described as a *Top Gun*-like take revolving around Starfleet Academy. They're digging the hole for the coffin before they even pull the plug on the body.

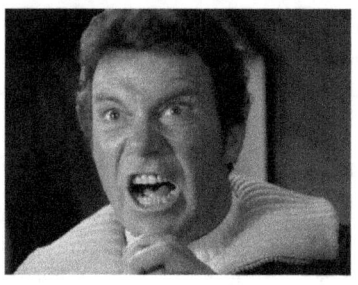

Here's my take: *Next Gen*'ers Levar Burton, Michael Dorn and Brent Spiner have expressed interest in moving on. The fans should get their chance to say good-bye, as opposed to some half-assed prequel.

After all, when characters die, the audience pays attention, even when they know there's a chance they'll re-appear in a flashback or on a holodeck down the line. What they do not want is something that bores them, as *Star Trek: Insurrection* did. When you've got Commander Riker piloting the whole damned ship with a videogame joystick, you know something's wrong.

The truth is that everything must come to an end. The folks in charge of *Star Trek's* destiny should stop off at their local video store and rent *Star Trek II: The Wrath Of Khan*. Spock tells us that the good of the many outweigh the good of the few.

Right now, the few are the Paramount bean counters concerned with cornering the next hip trend. Watching Paramount's political hot-stepping interfere with the creative process almost makes William Shatner's hambone over-emoting seem dignified.

Welcome to Enterprise

October 10, 2001

I like *Star Trek*, like anything else well done.

But *Deep Space Nine* and *Voyager* were uninspired spin-offs that added hours and hours of periods to a sentence finished long ago. Everyone in the galaxy seemed to be either neutered of any life whatsoever or forced to speak in some stylized rhetoric that would make a tribble cringe. Dominions, Cardassians, Ferengis. Phooey.

Gene Roddenberry's original *Trek* series was described as a wagon train to the stars. Give me strange new worlds and a swaggering cowboy captain any day next to the ponderous politically correct ensemble that boldly went nowhere.

I love shameless exploitation as much as the next guy, but not even Jeri Ryan in her skin-tight Borg cat suit was enough to make me tune in regularly. The whole thing was one big tired mess, and the addition of pin-up Ryan was just desperate.

The fans grew restless, calling for producer Rick Berman's head on a platter, claiming it was he who destroyed their precious franchise. Yet, the problem wasn't Berman or the writers so much as it was the corner they'd painted themselves into. Let's face it; the perfect world of the 24th century is pretty boring.

That's why *Enterprise*, the fifth series in the Trek canon is such a blast of fresh air. It takes place 100 years before Captain Kirk and only 150 years from now. In the world of *Enterprise*, people still swear, get scared, own dogs and enjoy an occasional drink. They watch movies and listen to music.

Heck, even the theme is a Rod Stewart stadium rock track. This isn't your father's *Enterprise*, it's ours.

And it's sexy without being desperate. Okay, maybe it was a *little* desperate in the opening episode when T'Pol (Jolene Blalock) had to grease herself down in that antibacterial chamber.

After all, the notion of space exploration and the first to fly *out there* is a very sexy idea, full of promise and adventure. That the Enterprise Science Office also happens to be a Vulcan hottie played by a Maxim pin-up girl only makes sense.

But unlike Jeri Ryan's Borg babe, Blalock's character is cleverly

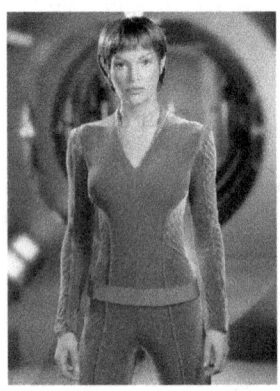

written as not only a cultural foil for our very human Captain Archer (Scott Bakula), but the source of all kinds of sexual tension.

Seems the Vulcans have held back the humans over the past century and Archer' harbors resentment. T'Pol is the personification of that conflict, but she also happens to be a babe. Add to that the Vulcans are a non-emotional lot and the pot heats to a simmer.

None of it would work if the dialogue wasn't clever. For that, Brannon Braga and Berman have the canvas of over 500 Trek hours to play connect-the-dots with, and by all accounts, they're having a blast. Let's hope the next seven years - if it lasts that long - holds true to the promise of the first two hour episode.

But we are talking about episodic television, in which the very nature of the format can work against any show. Sure, there are exceptions - *The West Wing* and *The Sopranos* come to mind - but unless the story keeps moving ahead, *Enterprise* runs the risk of becoming an "alien of the week" show. Let's hope it doesn't.

On the other side of the *Trek* fence is *Nemesis*, the hotly-contested tenth movie in the franchise, and the last to feature the crew of The *Next Generation*. The script, written by John Logan, attempts to be the greatest *Trek* movie since *The Wrath of Khan*, and doesn't make any bones about it, pardon the pun.

The script, which begins shooting next month under the direction of Stuart Baird, appears to have been leaked online. From all accounts, this last cinematic gasp may be as uninspired as *Enterprise* is filled with potential.

I won't reveal details, but I hope that the leaked script ends up being a ruse to fake everyone out. Logan may have written *Gladiator*, but let's not forget that he also wrote *Bats*.

If fictional Trek wasn't enough, November 6th brings the DVD release of *Mind Meld: Secrets Behind the Voyage of a Lifetime*, a taped conversation between Leonard Nimoy and William Shatner about mortality, alcoholism and their old pal DeForest Kelley.

The conversation disc coincides with the director's cut of *Star Trek: The Motion Picture* which features a remixed audio track and souped-up special effects.

There are no sure things in life, especially concerning the final frontier. But at least things are waking up in the *Trek* world and for better or worse, becoming more interesting.

And if that's not enough, they can always send Jolene Blalock back into that decontamination chamber.

POSTSCRIPT:
Enterprise floundered for its first two seasons, rebounded creatively for the next two and was canceled. The *Trek* universe lay dormant until Paramount signed J.J. Abrams to reboot the classic era of *Trek*. Fans grappled with the idea that someone else could possibly play Captain Kirk and Mr. Spock, but they got over it once the movie opened. Not only was it a critical hit, but it was also box office smash, netting $270 million.

Trek Keeps on Trekkin'

May 8, 2009

Well, who would have thunk it? This dynamic crowd-pleaser manages to serve as a sequel (to a *Next Generation* episode), prequel (to the classic original series) and reboot by way of some crafty storytelling.

Due to events in the opening sequence, the life of James T. Kirk (Chris Pine) is altered forever, forcing him to beat back his demons on his way to becoming captain of the starship Enterprise. But it's also a time-travel adventure (with Leonard Nimoy reprising his iconic role of Spock before handing it off to Zachary Quinto), a revenge flick, and an action movie, and *still* manages to find time for a dense back-story with some sexy retrofitting of the bridge crew's private lives.

This may be the first movie involving time travel in which the whole point was not fixing the timeline. And by not fixing it, there are a myriad of storytelling opportunities. Minor logic quibbles aside, this introduces us to the U.S.S. Enterprise's legendary crew by way of crisp characterizations and loving winks to the traits that made them legendary.

There isn't a single weak link, not the least of which: Quinto, who's half-human, half-Vulcan Spock has a lot to deal with; Zoe Saldana's Uhura is a complete (and sexy) reinvention as a fiercely intelligent and earthy presence. Karl Urban is Leonard McCoy incarnate and Simon Pegg's Scotty is (as always) the wild card.

Pine wisely elected to embody the heroic Captain Kirk as opposed to aping William Shatner. He's electrifying.

After ten films and (literally) hundreds of hours spanning five different series, Abrams and company pull off an impossible hat trick by making *Star Trek* cool again. Dare I say, energized?

Virtual Insanity
April 7, 1999

Science-fiction, by definition, starts with established scientific fact and leaps into the void from there. Exactly just how far or how convincing the leap, is dependent upon the storyteller. George Lucas and Michael Crichton have been particularly successful in grounding their tales in just enough reality to make it completely

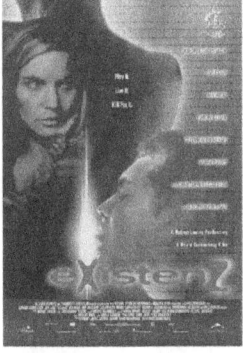

plausible that dinosaurs can walk the earth again, or that the force is with us.

In the 90's, virtual reality has often been considered the logical springboard for launching new and exciting sci-fi tales. But because the whole concept is so man-made and ethereal, nobody's really figured out a way to present it effectively. Even *The Lawnmower Man*, which was the first real attempt at creating drama from guys in chairs with things strapped to their bodies, never really quite pulled it off.

The problem lies in the concept. To deal with virtual reality as fiction is to start with the idea that in all of these stories - no matter how dangerous, sexy or spectacular a situation our heroes may find ourselves in, it always comes back to the fact that somewhere, characters are doing nothing more than lying still.

In the end, it might as well be a dream sequence.

In a few weeks, we'll continue this conversation as it applies to David Cronenberg's latest opus, *eXistenZ*, which opens April 23rd. I'll be respectful of the film's release date and not get into details, except to say that I saw both that film (pronounced ex-i-STENZ) and *The Matrix* the same day, and that Mr. Cronenberg's film didn't register much in comparison.

The Matrix is the highly-anticipated second film by Andy and Larry Wachowski, the wunderkind brothers who made a splash with the 1996 thriller *Bound*. The odds were leaning toward the brothers belly-flopping with a budget this high.

And let's face it, Warner Bros. hasn't exactly had good luck when it comes to marketing this sort of film lately. Barry Levinson's *Sphere* comes to mind.

But *The Matrix* is built around a great idea that finally manages to weave virtual reality elements through a narrative successfully. The idea is that what happens in cyberspace is reality; thereby making everything we know a fabrication. Add a plot that mixes equal parts *Terminator* and *Star Wars* and throw in some truly dazzling visuals, and you need a seat belt.

Even the much-maligned Keanu Reeves fares well here. Admit it: he's been good in his last few films, especially *The Devil's Advocate*, despite a reputation to the contrary. Reeves is an actor who has thrived in lower-budgeted films, but has made a smoother transition than, say, Nicolas Cage, to the Big Money Club. Strangely, shaved completely bald from head to toe, and covered in goo, Keanu looks right at home.

In *The Matrix*, Reeves is Neo, no less than The One chosen to battle the reality police of the Matrix. He displays the requisite amount of wonder, disbelief and "Whoa!"

All the performances are good, including Laurence Fishburne, at home in a role that's part warrior, part Obi-Wan.

The special effects are dazzling, but do not exist in a void. Yes, hard to believe, but the effects in *The Matrix* actually service the tale and move ahead the story.

And speaking of which, the Wachowski's made sure there was a story here - enough in fact for a few films. Details about the Matrix and Neo's destiny are ladled on thick in some early scenes, but considering that the brothers have announced there are two more *Matrix* stories to be told, that's not a bad thing.

I'd pay to see two more of these movies. There haven't been many good (and successful enough) first films to warrant sequels lately. A *Matrix* trilogy would be a nice little addition to a movie-going landscape that, over the next few years, is dotted with three *Star Wars* movies and a *Lord of the Rings* trilogy.

As for the whole virtual reality thing, we've still got the Cronenberg flick, and the similarly-plotted *The Thirteenth Floor*, which Sony has chosen to release May 28th opposite *Star Wars, Episode I: The Phantom Menace*.

Speaking of which. Six weeks and counting.

POSTSCRIPT:

Got a little ahead of myself there! *The Matrix* sequels were so overcooked and sloppy, they ruined the afterglow of the first film for me. Considering how precipitously the box office dropped after the second film, I guess I'm not alone. In retrospect, the coolest post-Matrix film in the series is *The Animatrix*, a series of animated short films done by different filmmakers in different styles.

X Appeal

July 19, 2000

James Cameron and Bryan Singer are two guys in Hollywood who need to sit down and drink a beer together. And I'd give up my autographed photo of Erin Gray to be a fly on the wall during that conversation.

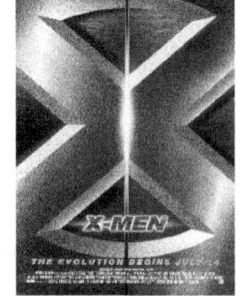

In 1989, Cameron's underwater adventure *The Abyss* was headed for a late July release date, but was nowhere near completed. There was no way Twentieth Century Fox was about to give up its plum July date for a silly little thing like making sure the film was actually done. Cameron patched up what he could, resulting in a truncated finale, middling reviews, and a mere $53 million box office. It would be four years until he would be able to actually complete the movie for a laserdisc release.

In 1997, Cameron's *Titanic* ran into the same problem, but Paramount decided to let the director have the time he needed to finish his $200 million opus. Needless to say, *Titanic* did okay.

Cut to 2000, and Fox has another hotly anticipated film on the schedule: Bryan Singer's $70 million adaptation of Marvel Comics' popular series *X-Men*. And like *The Abyss*, from 11 years earlier, Singer found himself staring down the film's impending July 14th release date with no possible opportunity for more time.

X-Men runs a scant 100 minutes, and just as I feared, the haste to make money on Fox's part has resulted in a film that will surely disappoint, if even on the slightest level.

Entire blocks of exposition are reduced to mere voice-over, action sequences lose key special effects, and the finale is rushed.

The premise, which is surprisingly dense with observations about the human condition, draws its fantasy elements from good old-fashioned human experiences like prejudice, fear, and alienation. Mutants are humans with spontaneously altered DNA that allows for certain gifts (or curses, depending on who you are). As the mutant population grows on earth, certain groups lobby for mutant identification, so that all the humans will know who all the mutants are, and would possibly seek to corral them together.

This none-too-subtle analogy between the growing feeling of uncertainly among the normal humans and the Nazis who prosecuted and killed Jews during World War II does not escape bad guy Magneto (a superb Ian McKellen), who was a child during the Holocaust. Magneto only wants to make the world safe for mutants, and that just may mean ridding the world of those pesky, inferior normal folks.

Incidentally, Magneto can alter all things of a metallic nature, so it doesn't matter that he's well into his 60's. He doesn't have to move fast, and is therefore a complex badass of a villain, certainly more interesting than the flamboyant baddies that inhabited Joel Schumacher's swishy *Batman* chapters.

Enter Logan/Wolverine (Hugh Jackman), a hunky brawler with a skeleton make of adamantium, an indestructible metal. The movie is seen through his eyes, and despite the presence of a star-studded cast of *X-Men*, the movie gets it right by following Logan through his journey. Jackman is charismatic, has all the best lines, and happens to be a good actor.

Especially good is Oscar-winner Anna Paquin, who plays Rogue, a teenage girl who loses the ability to make human contact with others (mere contact spontaneously draws the other's life force to her, making her stronger, but killing the other person). Needless to say, it makes dating on the difficult side.

Her solid performance isn't enough to make me take back any of the nasty things I said about her winning an Academy Award for *The Piano*, but at least she's finally backing that Oscar up. Funny that it took a comic book flick to get this good a performance out of her.

McKellen is good as always, but the rock of the film is Patrick Stewart as the wheelchair-bound Charles Xavier. Professor X is of the most powerful mutants on the planet, gifted with incredible telepathic powers that he can boost with his mind/computer interface, Cerebro. He and Magneto go way back and understand each other too well. It's a nice alternative to your average good guy/bad guy challenge.

Other mutants get as much time as the secondary crew in a *Star Trek* movie, but they are put to good use. On the evil side, shape shifter Mystique is a mostly nude blue-skinned Rebecca Romjin-Stamos. I knew that body-painting thing from Sports Illustrated's swimsuit issue a few years back could find its place in the world!

On Professor X's team are Jean Gray (Famke Jansen), the laser-eyed hothead Cyclops (James Marsden) and the beautiful Storm (Halle Berry) who can control the weather at will. Needless to say, Berry provides a refreshing dose of sex appeal.

It's apparent the filmmakers set out to not only appease the longtime fans of the comic, but to introduce newcomers as well. Having never read a frame of the strip, I was not confused for a moment about the mutants, the politics or the rather tricky relationships between characters.

I suspect that there's a double-disc DVD set looming on the horizon, which would presumably restore Singer's cut (rumored to be up to 30 minutes longer). Until then, fans of the film and comics have to settle for this surprisingly solid rush job.

Quick, get Magneto on the phone.

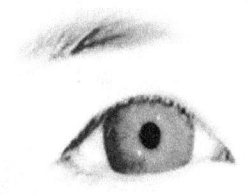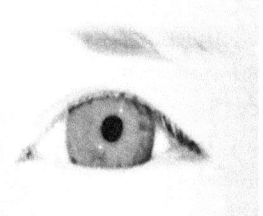

The Debate Over A.I.

July 11, 2001

A.I. Artificial Intelligence is having the exact effect on moviegoers that I thought it would. Most emerge confused, downright testy even. When pressed, as I have, truths emerge. It wasn't fast-paced enough. It wasn't happy enough. It was too disturbing for their kids.

Right, right and right.

But when push comes to shove, frustrated viewers finally have to admit that what they hated the most about *A.I.* was that it wasn't what they expected. But is that the movie's fault?

It's okay. Nobody liked *Blade Runner* in 1982 either, but now it's now regarded as a classic. And I'd pay good money to time warp back to 1968 to hear what people were saying after the head-scratcher that was Stanley Kubrick's *2001: A Space Odyssey*. (In case you've missed the headlines, Kubrick developed *A.I.* for two decades before he died. Steven Spielberg completed the project, based on Kubrick's extensive notes.)

I think *A.I.* will do alright in the grand scheme of things. For my money, it was of the most ambitious and boldest film issued by a major studio this year. It's rated PG-13, and no, it should not be seen by kids. There are images that last in the mind for days: a swimming pool sequence is not for anyone afraid of drowning.

Like Kubrick's *2001*, this film is ambiguous and bigheaded, offering an editorial on man ultimately losing out to machines when they are crafted too well. Unlike the other big dunderheaded movies out there, *A.I.* attempts to actually say something.

In the future, generations after robots (called mechas have been introduced as companions, workers, lovers, etc. A designer (William Hurt) sets out to design a mecha child, which would imprint to a family and love them forever.

His experiment, David, is played to perfection by 11-year old Haley Joel Osment. His new parents greet David with an uneasy curiosity, especially Frances O'Connor, who plays David's mommy, Monica Swinton. Of course, it's never explained why they couldn't just erase the kid's memory in the event things go wrong.

Some interesting ideas are explored in this episode, including the natural jealously between brothers, and the notion of blindly competing for the affections of a parent. In many ways, this first third is the most unsettling, because it takes organic dysfunctional relationships to a degree that simply shouldn't be tried at home.

The first third concludes in a horrifying way that propels our young hero on his quest for the blue fairy. David's new obsession becomes finding this mythical character from *Pinocchio*, in hopes that she will make him a real boy so his mommy will love him.

David has two companions, a sex mecha named Gigolo Joe (Jude Law) and a teddy bear named Teddy, who speaks in a deep, raspy voice. Law embodies his cocky sex robot with a verve that harkens back to Kubrick's *A Clockwork Orange*. He's amazing.

Through it all, there are strong glimpses of the directors' works: Spielberg's characters that yearn to belong *ala Close Encounters of the 3rd Kind* or *E.T.* and Kubrick's twisted societal observations that paint a bleak picture of humanity. There's a very interesting push-

and-pull between the different styles of the legendary auteurs that mostly compliment each other's oeuvre.

Like *2001*, the film ends with a final act that is a brave, puzzling leap. To reveal it would be unfair, but it should be said that it's during this sequence that worst of this unlikely collaboration becomes obvious.

Imagine *2001*'s grandiose statement about evolution if it came with a narrator that stopped the movie to make sure everybody got all nice and caught up.

Osment, for his immediate critical acclaim (and an Oscar nod) for *The Sixth Sense*, arrives with the confidence of the best actors of any age working in film. Law is sensational as the ladykiller droid and spouts his bravado with panache. Both deserve Oscar nominations.

The biggest problem with *A.I,* though, is that it was released in the heart of the summer movie season, when IQ points drop to the level of your average admission price. By holding the movie until December, the movie-going mood might have allowed for more thoughtful Oscar-friendly fare.

Some folks have given me a funny look when I tell them that I really liked this film. Why wouldn't I? It's brilliantly acted, has scene after scene filled with ideas and images I've never seen before, and with the exception of that spoon-fed finale, is challenging throughout.

If I want dumbed-down entertainment, I could simply go to *Tomb Raider*. Or *The Fast And The Furious*. Or *Scary Movie 2*. But I guess I stand mostly alone on this one.

It seems that in 2001, moviegoers definitely have a preference when choosing their summer entertainment: they'd rather it be artificial than intelligent.

6 THE BOOB TUBE

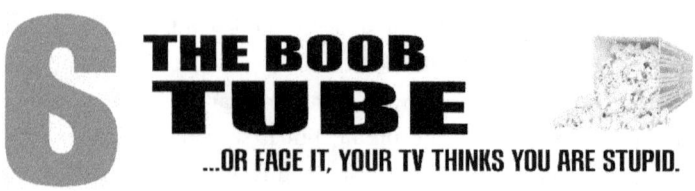

...OR FACE IT, YOUR TV THINKS YOU ARE STUPID.

No we're not talking about the sudden appearance of Janet Jackson's nipples at the Super Bowl in 2004, but it's ironic that any conversation about television in the first decade of the new century would include their mention.

Television has come a long way since 2000, when the major networks schedules became a wasteland of game shows and reality competitions. For a few years, it seemed to be a race to the bottom, not only in terms of ratings but our cultural dignity.

Thanks to the quality dramas on HBO, which crossed over into the mainstream far enough to start stealing major Emmys from the "big three," cable networks such as TNT, FX and USA began investing in storytelling again.

By mid-decade, TV seasons were boxed and sold on DVD; just a couple years later, viewers would begin devouring episodic TV on Amazon and Netflix. Now, it's a perfectly acceptable idea to find quality, original programming on those streaming services, as well as satellite providers such as DirecTV.

This brief collection of columns reflects my feelings about TV from a decade ago, and how the same "shoot first, blame someone else later" mentality had seeped into films in development.

This was before *Six Feet Under* and *The Sopranos* restored my faith, and years before the TiVo and Roku became the coolest things in the house.

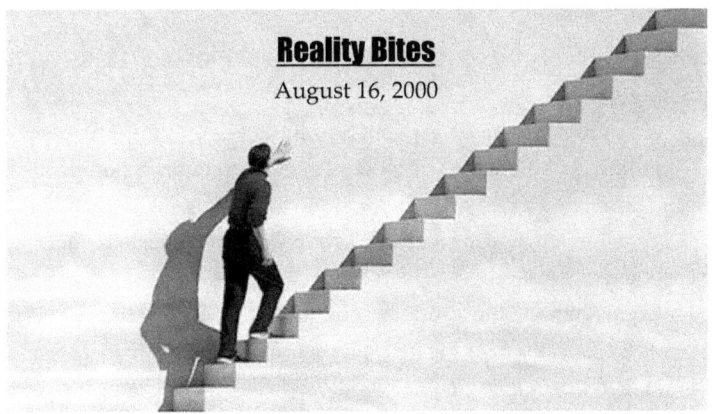

Reality Bites
August 16, 2000

When they said that the revolution will be televised, they weren't kidding. In a world in which casual camcorder use can produce shots of a flaming Concorde, it's really no surprise that the reality genre has finally paid off for the big networks.

But the folks who think CBS' *Survivor* and its counterpart *Big Brother* are innovations obviously haven't been watching much cable. Viacom's MTV (which now also owns CBS) has been pitting strangers against each other for a decade now on *The Real World*. Similarly, *Road Rules* features the same type of mixed bag of pissy athletic types, all competing against teams and each other.

Reality TV is big, and one needs to look no farther than his or her own webcam to see why. It's partly because the media has trained a nation of eager watchdogs to help them get fatter off the O.J. Simpsons and the Monica Lewinskys of the world. When Court TV and C-SPAN can make a name for themselves following the human condition as if it were an episodic soap opera, it makes me wonder what's next.

Wonder no more. CBS' surprise juggernaut *Survivor* is simply a reworked version of *The Real World*, except that the tribal council votes one of the castaways off the island on a weekly basis.

Considering what a pain in the ass he was for so long, Puck had it pretty good.

Let's face it, *Survivor* is about as genuine as *WWE's Smackdown*. Depending on how hours of footage gets cut into an action packed hour, different stories emerge. A sideways glance from Stacy and she's a bitch. A sweet comment from Colleen and she's melting hearts across the land.

Even Richard, the cantankerous nudist, probably has a better side than CBS is showing us, because in this narrative, he's the villain, so we get every snide, snotty, bitchy thing he says or does, including that fuzzy patch over his nether regions (which, we can only assume, is a good thing).

It's the crass and admittedly clever manipulation of these elements that have made *Survivor* what it is. It's an unabashed soap opera with real people. If the slightly more rambling *Big Brother* is missing any of *Survivor's* zing, it's because CBS airs the damned thing six times a week.

If the producers of *Big Brother* had taken a clue from, say, *The Real World*, they'd know there's more bang for your buck when an episode consists of a weekly highlight reel of mood swings and confessionals. And lose the studio audiences, fer heaven's sake: this isn't *The Truman Show*. Wait, maybe it is.

Thus far, the only drama on *Big Brother* was effectively eliminated when Jordan the stripper was voted out of the house. Now the biggest mystery is how long it will be until the flatulent dog clears the room again. People complain that the show is boring. No kidding: You may like your friends, but try pointing a camera at them for an hour and watching it back.

I've said it before and I mean it more even now. We live in a nation of rubberneckers, who feel their lives are not complete unless they know everything about your business. *Big Brother* is indeed watching, and we, my fellow Americans, are Big Brother.

And the hits just keep on coming. Mark Burnett, *Survivor's* demigod, might follow up his island adventure with *Destination Mir*, in which the winner - you guessed it - gets to go into space. In the end, Burnett will be credited with spurning a television revival, but will we, as a viewing nation, be the better for it?

The success of *Survivor* and *Big Brother* close a sort of loop in the de-evolution of our broadcast media. How far can it go, and what is the obvious conclusion? Who knows?

Is it entertaining? Sure, the way that listening in on someone's conversation provides a nasty little thrill, in the hopes they may do or say something worth repeating.

Everybody laughed when *The Truman Show* presented a twisted reality in which everyone in the world watched one man's life without him knowing. Now, the concept is commonplace, but our Trumans are willing participants. It's life imitating art, and edited together into a slick package.

Two weeks ago, the GOP convention inspired some of NBC's lowest ratings ever, and there's no telling if the Democrats can pull any more viewers. But here's an idea for NBC: Follow the candidates around, *Real World* style, through the ups and down, and every nasty little phase of the election.

Expose our presidential hopefuls as the human beings that they are, lay a hip soundtrack over the top, and turn *Election* into a weekly series. The winner doesn't just get a million bucks… he gets to be president.

Makes you wonder what George W. might say to the camera in the Red Room.

Look Closer

June 14, 2000

I used to look at sports writers and wonder how they could wield such sarcasm and vitriol on such a regular basis without really alienating their faithful readers. It was because most of the time, they made perfect sense.

When I prepare these columns for general consumption, there's not a time that I don't wonder whether I'm being a little too hard on the people and studios I'm writing about. All I can say is that like the sports writers, certain things just make perfect sense to me.

I'm rarely surprised when a film, musical act or television show rises to the top or crashes badly. To quote *American Beauty's* brilliant ad campaign, all you have to do is look closer.

It's amazing to me that nobody in the entertainment industry bothers looking closer at anything. The entire industry seems to operate from an ego-driven case of denial, enabled by development costs and salary perks. The challenge should be to spot what works and what doesn't *before* it goes into pre-production.

But in Hollywood, developing movies and TV shows that actually make creative and financial sense isn't Mission: Difficult, it's Mission: Impossible.

Thank the maker Nicolas Cage has finally decided to pass on playing Superman (face it, he would have looked ridiculous in the blue tights). This is only after Warner Bros. invested a reported *$100 million* into development costs and several high-profile rewrites.

Maybe they should have spent a tenth of that money to give the Superman fans what they really want: a digitally remastered version of Richard Donner's 1978 classic *Superman*. Restore the legendary missing scenes, slap it on a widescreen DVD and actually get some mileage from the fact that 1998 would have been the 60th anniversary of the comic, and the 20th anniversary of the film.

But no, that would have made too much sense. Warner was so interested in developing a summer movie thrill ride that they missed the point entirely.

Kevin Smith's animated *Clerks* was canned after two episodes on ABC. Smith had long since pronounced the show stillborn after being shuffled all over ABC's landscape and finally dumped into the summer schedule on Tuesdays.

The critics loved it, the audiences dug it, but leave it to the brilliant minds at the Asinine Broadcasting Company to decide it was too edgy for them. Maybe they could have simply let it go to another network, as opposed to piddle all over it they way they did, but now, it's damaged goods, and the suits at the Mouse House got their perfect revenge for Smith's regular blasting of the studio on his website, viewaskew.com. More power to him, and here's hoping the episodes become available for download soon.

In *Star Trek* news, anticipating is slowly starting to build for *Voyager's* final season, which will most likely see the ship finally return home. There will also be a tenth *Trek* flick that will be more high adventure than the cerebral *Star Trek: Insurrection.*

The idea is to have a high concept balls-out actioner, similar to the gritty *First Contact*. Never has a film series had to fix itself as much as *Trek*. Every even-numbered installment seems to be an apology of sorts for the misfire that was an odd-numbered one. But there's that marketing thing again.

CBS is loudly celebrating their *Survivor* victory against ABC's *Who Wants To Be A Millionaire*. That's like Outback Steak House celebrating that they got the meat lover who's finally sick of eating salads. Duh! *Millionaire* airs, like, forty-seven times a week. Of course audiences are eventually going to get burned out.

CBS did the right thing by putting their *Real World* meets *Gilligan's Island* opus against the Philbinator. Heck, when Regis himself starts to look like 39 days on a deserted island might not be a bad thing, you gotta wonder if maybe ABC isn't riding the *Millionaire* horse a little hard.

Richard Gere and Julia Roberts have finally agreed to do *Pretty Woman 2*, but both want $20 million and director Frank Marshal wants $10 mil. That's $50 million just in salaries. Roberts and Gere make a great screen couple, but *Runaway Bride* should have satisfied any need to go back to the *Pretty Woman* well again.

We'll end with the sole glimmer of common sense on display in Hollywood last week. Mike Myers turned his back on a $20 million salary and his commitment to make *Dieter* because he just wasn't able to make the script work. Universal promptly sued him, to which he responded with a counter suit and the following statement: "I cannot in good conscience accept $20 million and cheat moviegoers who pay their hard-earned money to see my work by making a movie with an unacceptable script."

Bravo, Mike. That's the kind of thinking that could have saved the world from a *Battlefield Earth* or a *Viva Rock Vegas*. Dr. Evil might not approve, but I'm sure his fans ultimately will.

POSTSCRIPT: It's always interesting looking back on the deals that made big news. Cage never made *Superman* but 2006's *Superman Returns* was a critical failure, despite hewing so closely to Donner's original film. *Pretty Woman 2* never happened, and *Nemesis* was the last film before a rousing 2009 *Star Trek* reboot. Also, *Dieter* never got made, but that didn't stop Myers from inflicting *The Love Guru* onto an unsuspecting world. Where was his good conscience on that one?

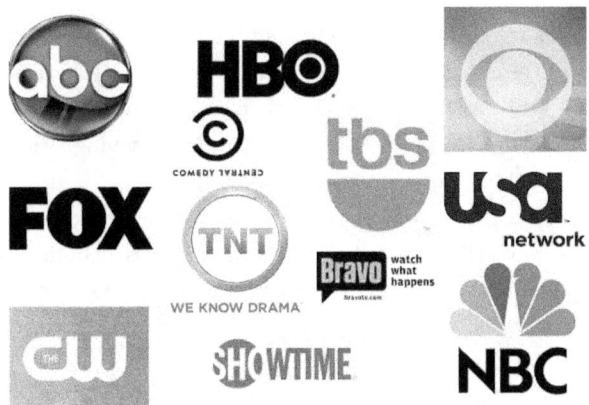

Teeveenomics
February 6, 2006

It's ironic that while so many studios are successfully exploring alternate ways to create revenues for their catalogs of shows, that the Big Four networks are as desperate as ever to try to cut costs. Despite DVD box sets, downloadable episodes on iTunes and DirecTV's eventual sneak preview tier that will allow viewers to watch advance episodes of their favorite shows for $3.99 a pop, the networks are still up to their old tricks.

NBC recently cancelled *The West Wing* after seven seasons and umpteen awards. Fox's *Arrested Development* is benched and likely cancelled, but because of interest from other networks, the death certificate has not been filled out. UPN killed *Star Trek: Enterprise* just when it started getting good. *King of the Hill* quietly shut down production and *Will and Grace* concludes in May.

What do all these shows have in common, aside from being bumped off? Their networks will tell you it is their low ratings. But the truth is more alarming: the shows were expensive to produce and recently relocated to another night, generally one with brutal competition (Sunday) or one with no viewers at all (Friday or Saturday). When a show costs $3 million an episode and there are contracts in play, the network has an easy out by saying, "Hey, we believe in the show, but nobody's watching it!"

This is most typical of star-driven vehicles. Ever wonder why the new sitcom with a once-big Hollywood star is debuting on a Thursday night, opposite a crush of programming? It's usually not because a network is super-confident. It's because the show is easy to kill if the ratings are low.

Remember *Max Headroom*, the late 80's TV satire? In that near-future scenario, shows were cancelled mid-episode if the ratings weren't good enough. The funny thing about satire is that it eventually always comes true.

Heather Graham's *Emily's Reasons Why Not* was dumped after one episode. *The Night Stalker* after a half dozen. *Reunion* was a great idea - a mystery spanning 20 years over twenty episodes, but Fox launched it on Thursday nights and cancelled it after about 10 episodes, meaning that nobody will ever find out how it ends.

In March, *Las Vegas* will move to Friday. Guess what that means? The ratings will drop and the flashy James Caan starrer (read: expensive) will be gone by the end of the season. Ditto *Boston Legal*, with James Spader and William Shatner. Both are award-winning stars and the show has some buzz, but the Tuesday numbers are down. I give it one more year, tops.

Ever wonder why reality shows are so prolific? It's a happy accident that people actually *watch* them. Truth is, when you can get an entire season of *The Amazing Joe Bachelor's Survivor Race* for the same price as an episode of *ER*, the economics of it all has some appeal in the board room.

If it's truly about the ratings, riddle me this: with all the DVR viewing and On Demand options, why does Neilson only count the ratings of the show when it airs live?

Two years ago, TiVo reported that the Janet Jackson boob flash was the most replayed event in their history. If a company can report a 180 percent spike for a moment lasting less than a second, they can certainly count how many times *Arrested Development* was watched last week. Why don't those numbers count?

Maybe it's because the networks don't want those numbers to count. Let's say three million people watched *Star Trek: Enterprise* but another five million watched it on TiVo (go with me, kids, I'm making a point), then at some point, UPN has to consider the TOTAL amount of viewers, not just the ones that might prove their point about low numbers to justify cancellations.

The big networks can only get away with this for so long. In less than a decade, everything will be on demand, just like movie trailers on the internet.

When that happens, when the scales are tipped so that nobody feels the need to watch television live anymore, then that's when the true picture will emerge. The clicks don't lie, which is why the big companies hate them.

But the smaller networks - HBO, FX, Sci-fi, etc. - are the ones with exciting programs. Their seasons generally last 13 weeks vs. the big networks' 26 and with less time to fill, the storytelling is just tighter. The seasons are easily boxed and sold; DVD box sets have become the currency of reruns. The big networks can learn a thing or two about how the smaller guys develop and package their shows.

When done right, a season can represent a series of chapters in an ongoing tale. Viewers get that. Shows premiere on TV and are packaged onto DVD. Viewers can then buy them or rent them at their local video store, like any other form of entertainment.

Given this, why didn't Fox shoot all the episodes of *Reunion* before stiffing it? They could have premiered the episodes on the internet, shuttled them to FX, or gone straight to DVD. To add insult to injury, Fox recently revealed the would-be ending in a press release. If you missed it, Samantha's murderer was the illegitimate daughter she fathered with Will.

Classy move, Fox.

To kill a show like that in mid-story isn't just random and careless, it's downright rude to the people who were asked to invest time into it in the first place. You mean to tell me that Fox couldn't shift some of that *American Idol* revenue to cover *Reunion's* back?

Sure, they could have.

Television had better figure out its game plan. With so many evolving ways for people to enjoy their filmed entertainment and with home theaters and declining admissions contributing to the rise in home viewings, the networks have a golden opportunity here: to begin treating their audiences with respect.

But we all know that will never happen.

On a final note, the recent decision to merge The WB and UPN is brilliant, if the newly minted The CW plays to its strengths. A network with a line-up that includes *Smallville, Veronica Mars, Everybody Hates Chris, Gilmore Girls, Everwood* and *Supernatural* could be a real contender. But that name, short for CBS (UPN's parent company) and WB, is a loser. They couldn't agree on something catchier?

Tell you what, guys - you can keep the name but put in a bid for *Arrested Development* and all will be forgiven.

Why TV Sucks

March 8, 2000

Let me count the ways. But first, take this pop quiz. Out of all the major networks, which one has quietly vaulted to fifth place behind ABC, NBC, CBS and Fox?

The answer, when we return from our rant.

As we move closer and closer to an internet teeming with streaming media, the question begs: What has TV done for us lately? Well, aside from a recently reported increase in commercial ads clogging the airwaves (17 minutes per hour), and water cooler classics such as that whole *Multi-Millionaire* fiasco, not a whole lot.

First, let's address the blight that was *Who Wants To Marry A Multi-Millionaire,* and why it dragged the boob tube down a few more IQ points. To recap, the multi-millionaire was slapped with a restraining order, and the bride never served in the Gulf War. But she so badly wants the nation to know that she made an error in judgment, she appears on *Good Morning America,* and cries her little eyes out. Somehow, I know all of this and never watched a frame of the show, or its media blitz.

The bride didn't make an error in judgment; it was a desperate spasm for attention. The poor girl probably wasn't hugged enough as a child. But she does get a lovely parting gift of $35,000 and a new truck. That's a fair trade off.

Just as Monica Lewinsky is hawking Jenny Craig products and showing up regularly on *Extra* (that beacon of journalist integrity), these poor folks cling to that 15 minutes of fame so tightly, they taint everything around them. Go away, fer heaven's sake!

Of course, Fox has stated formally that reality-based shows will be banned forever. Except *Cops,* of course. And those Robbie Knievel specials. You can also forget about that special in which they were going to crash an unoccupied 747 in the desert.

But that's not going to stop Twentieth TV, a subsidiary of Fox from producing a syndicated show called *I Do, I Don't*, in which couples looking to get married in Las Vegas can get talked out of it by an audience. Fear not, rubberneckers. The WB and UPN have made no such proclamations. They're not above a little good old-fashioned exploitation.

The network numbers are all at record lows, save for ABC's *Who Wants To Be A Millionaire*, the show that single-handedly united the world. But its meteoric success says much for our falling IQ's. Since the first eight questions or so are no-brainers, we revel in high-fiving each other and screaming at our TV's. "The answer is *Star Trek*, you idiot!" Guilty as charged.

Remember the good old days when people actually had to know things to win big bucks on a quiz show? NBC's *Twenty One*, was once scandal-plagued for giving the contestants the answers before airtime, and was taken off the air. But they're not quiz shows anymore. They're multiple-choice shows.

It's all going to hell in a hand basket, folks. A recent watchdog survey of the Bay Area newscasts rated KGO, KRON and KPIX all with D+'s, due to their reliance on 911 Stories (KTVU's newscast earned a B+ for airing more stories that explored issues).

Similarly, CBS (The Tiffany Network!) is trying hard to snag the WWE from The USA network. Then again, this is the same network that dared to show a movie about JonBenet Ramsey called *Perfect Murder, Perfect Town*. It was number one in its time slot the night it aired, and to all of you who contributed by watching...

Shame on you.

By the way, the fifth-largest network (by viewership) in the United States is now Telemundo.

7 NOTEWORTHY DIRECTORS
...AND THE MOVIES THAT MADE THEM WORTH THE HYPE.

When it comes to artists who "define a generation," beauty is in the eye of the beholder.

Nirvana may have epitomized the angst of the 90s as an expression of lost youth and misguided culture, but others can relate more to the soothing tones of Celine Dion.

To each, their own.

When it comes to "definitive lists" of the best this or that, let's face it: they are all hooey. But they inspire discussion, dissention and self-analysis. And they're fun!

This is not a definitive list as much as an informal vertical sampling of reviews and articles that illuminate (in my humble opinion) some of the strongest voices of this generation, and movies that struck a chord.

I am quite aware that there are so many more filmmakers that deserve mention, artists that I not only admire, but await their next projects anxiously.

But there is only so much space.

So, apologies to Richard Linklater, Joel and Ethan Coen, Steven Soderbergh, Errol Morris, Michael Winterbottom, Paul Thomas Anderson, Wes Anderson, Ang Lee and Lars von Trier. Certainly, you shall all be better represented in the next *American Popcorn* book

Away we go...

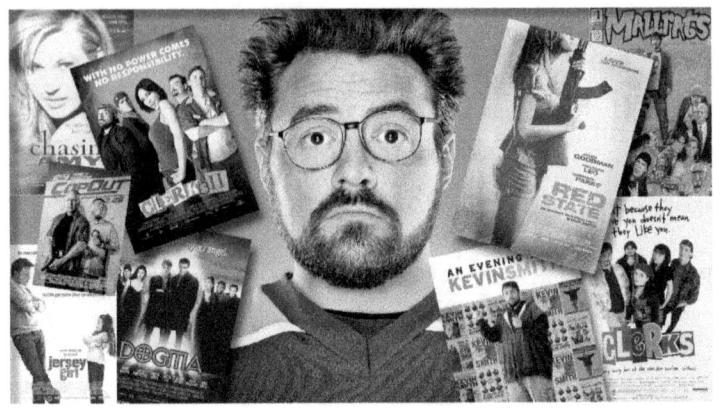

KEVIN SMITH

Kevin Smith, by his own admission, is one of the luckiest SOBs to ever hold a camera or be blessed enough to have a career. But I think it's much more than that. Smith came of age during the wave of independent cinema that rose during the early 90s, armed with a secret weapon that would serve him better than ambition, or even skill. He had honesty on his side.

His dialogue, however crude, was refreshingly frank. His characters, however limited in their worldview, grappled with weighty subjects as love, fidelity, insecurity, and faith. You might not have realized it at the time, but *Clerks* (1994), *Clerks II* (2006) and *Chasing Amy* (1997) all had big things to say about growing up; *Zack and Miri Make a Porno* (2008) is an unabashed love story.

Yes, there was filler, and even a big studio gig, *Cop Out* (2010), that netted him his worst reviews (and biggest grosses). But Smith has always made sure his "dick and fart" movies have had a little more going on under the hood.

There may be no other media figure with a following as devoted as his. The ardent support of his fans (and fellow filmmakers) has allowed Smith to flourish in many careers: film writer and director, comic book writer, producer, radio host, on-stage provocateur and internet radio personality. He is also self-deprecating, gracious, eager to interface with fans (in person and on Twitter), and a walking pop culture encyclopedia.

Arguably, *Red State* (2011) was Smith's greatest evolution as a filmmaker and distributor. By subverting the studio system and touring with the film, he created a paradigm shift in the way films could be experienced in the 21st century. *Red State* was about the fallibility of cult mentality and, and Smith followed that thought all the way through to its ultimate, bloody conclusion.

But his first, unabashed reach for the brass ring was *Dogma* (1999), an ambitious, if flawed rumination on faith that ruffled a great many feathers, and saw its released delayed several times.

Although *Dogma* was borne out of Smith's own questions about (and celebration of) Catholicism, it's understandable that the controversy (and death threats) that preceded its release would have planted the seeds for what would eventually become *Red State*.

The Last Temptation Of Smith
November 17, 1999

Dogma comes with baggage, most of it undeserved, but expected. Dumped by Miramax (and Disney) for being a controversial hot potato and rescued by Lionsgate, *The Little Religious Satire That Could* has incurred the wrath of bible-pounding Catholics and purists alike ... without having even been seen.

But in its full glory, *Dogma* delivers a message that tells people to find some sort of faith ... or better, an idea ... and embrace it, because God gave you that choice.

Now, I ask you, how offensive is that message, when compared to recent sub-plots in movies like *Vampires* or *Stigmata*, which suggests all kinds of nefarious dealings concerning the Catholic Church? Even The Mole's anti-God rants in *South Park: Bigger, Longer and Uncut* were far more shocking.

Dogma tells the story of two fallen angels, Bartleby (Ben Affleck) and Loki (Matt Damon), who were banished to Earth eons ago. They have discovered a dogmatic loophole that would allow them to return to Heaven: all they have to do is travel from Wisconsin to New Jersey and pass through the arches of an infamous cathedral, in which Cardinal Glick (George Carlin) has kicked off a campaign to make Catholicism hip, complete with a thumbs-up Buddy Christ.

Bethany (Linda Fiorentino) finds herself visited by Metatron (Alan Rickman), the angel who serves as God's voice. Metatron has a dire assignment. He must convince Bethany, who has long since lost her faith, to take up the mission to stop Loki and Bartleby from entering the church, and thereby erasing existence.

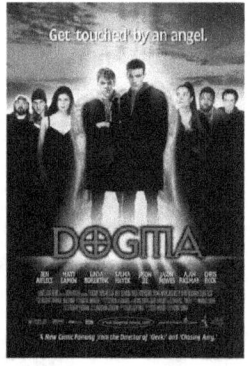

After prophets Jay and Silent Bob (Kevin Smith's ever-present comic duo; Bob is played by Smith himself) make themselves available for the jaunt to Jersey, they come across Rufus, the 13th apostle, who happens to be black, and is still steamed at the Bible's racial injustices, and a muse named Serendipity (Salma Hayek) who doubles as a stripper.

Smith uses this canvas for every theory about organized religion and faith he could muster, some thought-provoking, some infantile. But most of the time, I was thinking how cool it was that someone had the balls to make these statements.

The Apocalypse and the Catholic Church have rarely been anything more than devices for bad horror movies, so Smith's take is refreshing. Judging from the funny, but somewhat defensive title cards that open this film, Smith is all too aware of the storm he's brewed.

The performances are wonderful, even when the material is less than fleshed out. Linda Fiorentino's Bethany is a great anti-heroine with a confused fierceness that allows for moments of regret and anger. Alan Rickman brings a wry approach to his reluctant messenger, and Chris Rock, finally gets to do something other than rant. Alanis Morissette makes a late appearance as a goofy God, and for having no dialogue, does it perfectly.

Matt Damon and Ben Affleck, last seen together in the definitive *Good Will Hunting* are no less solid here. What could have been done with a wink toward satire, they play straight, and it's a good call. There's a dramatic scene in which Affleck's benign angel reassesses his position against God that makes just enough sense to be the most frightening scene in the film.

The irony is that Kevin Smith coerces great performances from his heavyweight cast but seems unable to capture the grandeur of his message. He spends a good portion of the film *telling* us more than he does *showing* us. Smith's best asset is that he's a great writer: funny when he needs to be, subtle when it's appropriate and serious when the material calls for it.

But with every film, he proves my theory more and more: Smith should write his films and hire someone to call the shots. It's nice to be a hyphenate filmmaker, but Smith did everything here but sing the closing theme (at least he let Morissette handle that).

The original cut of *Dogma* weighed in at three hours, and now it's a leaner 135 minutes. Granted things hop along nicely at times, but it's still too long. Come on, Kevin, it never occurred to you to cut the "shit monster" sequence to tighten things up?

God willing, one day, Kevin Smith will be considered a brilliant filmmaker, and might actually win an Academy Award for his writing. But something tells me the script he wins an Oscar for won't feature a demon made of feces.

QUENTIN TARANTINO

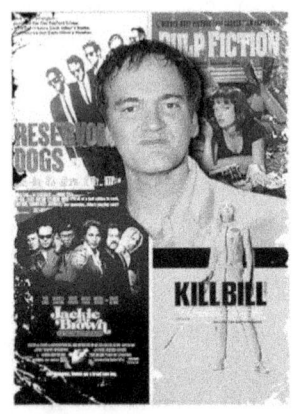

One need not know the history of cinema (circa the early 90's) to know the impact Quentin Tarantino has had on the industry. No other director in modern times has been as hyped, debated, dissected and imitated.

Tarantino struck fast and hard, writing a series of catchy crime flicks that lived inside a self-contained universe. *Reservoir Dogs. True Romance. Pulp Fiction. Natural Born Killers.* All within two years.

He followed *Pulp Fiction* (1994) with *Jackie Brown* (1997), an adaptation of an Elmore Leonard novel, proving he had good taste. He contributed to buddy Robert Rodriguez' *Desperado* (1995) and co-directed *Four Rooms* (1996). An unfortunate detour into acting and self-parody followed. Say what you will about thespian Tarantino's range, but it's worth pointing out that he and future Oscar-winner George Clooney co-starred in the same horror movie together, *From Dusk Till Dawn* (1996).

Self-professed movie geek Tarantino is well aware of the most famous line from the *Spider-man* films: "With great power, comes great responsibility." QT has used that power to resurrect the careers of John Travolta, Daryl Hannah, David Carradine, Don Johnson, Pam Grier, Kurt Russell, and the great Robert Forster.

I think Uma Thurman, Samuel L. Jackson, Ving Rhames, Michael Madsen, Steve Buscemi, Christoph Waltz, and Michael Fassbender would also agree that a debt of gratitude is owed him.

Tarantino's name remained off-screen for six years until he returned with *Kill Bill* (2003), a movie audaciously released in two parts, each equally successful. *Kill Bill* led Tarantino into B-movie waters up to his neck. He directed *Death Proof* (2007), which was technically the second-half of a two-part "double feature" called *Grindhouse*, which bombed at the box office.

For a while, he appeared resigned to roll around in the kinds of exploitation fare he loved so much as an impressionable filmgoer. *Death Proof* featured an incredible finale with a speeding car stunt so insane, it's worth the price of admission.

But it all seemed like a step backward.

Until, of course, Tarantino released *Inglourious Basterds* (2009), a revisionist fantasy that rewrote the ending of World War II and displayed as much restraint as *Kill Bill* severed limbs.

Basterds was the culmination of Tarantino's evolution as a filmmaker. It had the lived-in realism of *Pulp Fiction*, the savagery of *Reservoir Dogs*, the grown-up emotional duplicity of *Jackie Brown*, and the technical proficiency of *Kill Bill.*

Although it was hard to realize at the time, *Kill Bill* was the hinge film, the seemingly cartoonish throwaway that slung him into the second phase of his career. Here are my thoughts at the time, along with my review of *Basterds* and an Examiner article I wrote about the night Tarantino came to San Francisco.

And lemme tell you, watching a movie *with* Tarantino is an amazing experience!

Kill Bill: Thrills and Shills

October 15, 2003

Kill Bill is the ultimate in geek worship. Just as countless first-timers have aped QT's hip dialogue and pop culture references, the first half of Tarantino's 4th film is a little more than a masturbatory love letter to the grind-house chop-sockey fare he grew up watching.

You know, I watched a lot of *Godzilla* movies but if I were a filmmaker, I wouldn't feel the need to subject the world to 3 hours and 20 minutes of a guy in a rubber suit stomping on plastic cities.

That's right. *Kill Bill* is 3 hours and 20 minutes.

But instead of hiring an editor, Miramax and Tarantino have decided that *Kill Bill* needed to be two movies. Until I saw the first half, I thought this was a terrible idea.

But the action sequences are rather gruesome and *Volume 2* has all the great character stuff Tarantino has built his empire on. In theory, giving audiences a four month break and rewarding them with classic QT stuff might be the way to go.

That is, unless, people find *Volume 1* too cold, too violent, and too much of nothing at all. It's a huge risk, but if it works, expect more self-indulgent 3-hour films to be split in half rather than simply editing the thing. Can you imagine if *Pulp Fiction, Volume 1* ended with Butch shooting Vincent?

Kill Bill concerns a pregnant woman (Uma Thurman) left at the alter for dead after – and I'm not making this up – her former assassination squad performed a hit on her. She wakes up five years later and sets out to kill everyone involved, including her boss and lover, Bill (David Carradine)

I'd love to tell you her name but Tarantino thought it would be cute to bleep it out every time someone says it, only to reveal it in *Volume 2*. Aw, the hell with it. Her name is Beatrix Kiddo. Bet your friends and thank me later.

All this assassination squad stuff is basically *Fox Force Five*, the TV pilot Uma's *Pulp Fiction* character famously acted in, but you probably already figured that out.

Volume 1 is all about style, considering it doesn't have much in the way or character or story to fall back on just yet. We're talking stylized violence punctuated with boom-chacka-laka beats on the soundtrack or a tinny B-movie sample whenever Uma goes krakatoa on someone's ass. It's cute at first, but grows tiresome as the violence escalates and limbs begin flying.

One particularly bloody combat sequence is mostly in black and white, and I suspect that's the only reason *Kill Bill* squeaked by with an R rating. With writing bodies and a sea of spurting blood, the scene goes from being absurdly violent to disturbing.

Thurman is very good, especially in the moments that she's allowed some leeway to act like a human being. Karate legend Sonny Chiba (a favorite of *True Romance's* Clarence) appears as a sword maker. Lucy Liu doesn't do much but she's better here than she's ever been before, and others – Michael Madsen, Daryl Hannah and David Carradine – all get their choice scenes in Part Deux.

Chiaki Kuriyama steals every moment as a lethal killer with a nasty ball-and-chain act who dresses like a uniformed school girl. Her name is Go-Go and that's what the movie does when she's onscreen. Julie Dreyfus, not to be confused with Seinfeld's pal, does a lot with very little screen time.

To his credit, Tarantino infused his action sequences with some impressive gravity-defying wire work and choreography. But how many times can the whoosh of a blade and the hose-spraying of blood be effective?

Kill Bill might emerge as a cult favorite once it can be seen as one complete film. But *Volume 1* stands as a blatant reminder that movies should not be released by the slice. Unlike the impact Reservoir Dogs and Pulp Fiction had on a wave of young filmmakers, I can't imagine anyone wanting to emulate anything in this film. But it's still better than *Things To Do In Denver When You're Dead*.

Volume 2
April 16, 2004

The last-minute decision to chop Quentin Tarantino's *Kill Bill* into two halves will be debated for many moons. On the surface, the decision seems justified: *Volume 2* is so tonally different than the violent cartoon that was *Volume 1* that it feels like a completely different experience. However, there are strands of story and character arcs that pay off brilliantly in the finale that are almost lost in the time that passes between viewing the separate volumes.

Tarantino's great gamble will one day result in a combined version that will see *Kill Bill* as one, long, physically and emotionally exhausting yarn that will attain the type of cult status it deserves.

Volume 1 seemed empty, devoid of any characters worth caring about. *Volume 2* breaks new Tarantino ground with the most fully realized adult relationships in his resume. And yes, that includes the delightfully grown-up *Jackie Brown*.

The Bride aka Beatrix Kiddo (Uma Thurman) may be a lean, mean killing machine, but like *Pulp Fiction's* aforementioned Jules (Samuel L. Jackson), she is presented with a choice that forever alters her destiny.

I would never dream of revealing the fact that Kiddo's daughter still lives at the time of this revenge, but seeing how *Volume 1* tossed it out there like a cheap cliffhanger, so be it (in the shooting script, the twist was held until the very end).

Thurman looks great when she's Kung Fu Fightin' but she's also amazing in her tender moments – glancing at Bill like he's the greatest thing that ever happened to her, exploring a sacred relationship with her 4-year-old daughter, or even rectifying her violent past as she attempts to segue to a life as a record store clerk on the day of her wedding.

We all know that the wedding party turned into a shooting party, and by now, if you've seen *Volume 1,* you know who's left on her list: Bill's brother Budd (Michael Madsen) and the venomous one-eyed Elle (Daryl Hannah).

And Bill, that smooth-talking, villainous son of a bitch who started it all by daring to care about Beatrix. Bill is played by David

Carradine in a role originally designed for Warren Beatty. Almost as perplexing as lopping *Kill Bill* into two movies was Beatty opting out and recommending Carradine for the role. Carradine chews it up, never once taking Bill into parody.

He's slick, charming and he'll always surprise you. He's James Bond gone wrong. It's a pity this two-movie approach wasn't enough to include a chapter from the script called *Can She Bake A Cherry Pie,* which existed to introduce us to Bill's world.

When he shows up at the beginning of *Volume 2*, his chemistry with Uma Thurman is palpable. The scene is long and talky, and as history unfolds and familiarity sets in, we forget that in a few moments, he will unleash holy hell on The Bride and her happy day.

Kill Bill is yet another example of Tarantino's unbeatable ability to match the perfect actor to a great character for a career-best performance. When was the last time Daryl Hannah did anything worthy of mention? Here, she's a classic villain with a nasty method of getting her way. Ditto Budd (Madsen), who delivers the ominous line: "That woman deserves her revenge, and we deserve to die."

There are a lot of great lines in *Volume 2*. In fact, the best compliment I can pay this half a film is that it's a Tarantino flick, complete with great characters, surprising moments, quotable dialogue and a flow that goes against the grain of what almost any other auteur would have delivered.

It has been said that he is obsessed with Uma Thurman. It would be hard to argue that point given how gloriously he has elevated everything about her for this double feature. But he has also given Thurman no less than one of the best roles ever conceived for a woman – fierce, loving, motherly and deadly – all on her own terms. Beatrix Kiddo lives and breathes and cries and does the things we all wish we could. It's an amazing performance.

QT delivers the goods, but he's so in love with his own film, he just can't let go. There are no less than four credit rolls that take up the last 15 minutes of the movie. Curiously, every major player – in order of appearance, starting with the actors in *Volume 1*, all get full screen shots and credit. I suspect that once the volumes are glued back together that this bombastic sequence will stand as the definitive player shout-out.

Tarantino may be the most pretentious writer-director working today. And given the crap that passes for studio entertainment, that is a compliment. I think of the absolute onslaught of QT wannabe's that flooded cineplexes in the wake of *Pulp Fiction*.

Sure, we bemoan those dark ages as the result of flaccid studio copycatting, but take a look around at this industry where McG, Jan De Bont and Michael Bay are handed $100 million budgets to deliver generic CGI action instead of any semblance of plot.

Was it really so bad then?

Quentin Tarantino rocks San Francisco's Castro Theater
August 21, 2009

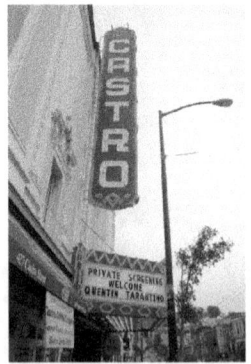

Iconic director Quentin Tarantino brought his *Inglourious Basterds* to San Francisco's famed Castro Theater for a lively premiere and Q&A session on Wednesday night.

The auteur's sixth film is set during World War II with interlocking stories about a terror squad meant to shake up the Third Reich; and a young woman whose family was slaughtered. She now runs the movie theater where the Nazis want to premiere their latest propaganda film.

Prior to the screening, the internal scuttlebutt had been that Tarantino was exhausted from a Q&A screening in Chicago (and a two-hour flight delay). But you'd never have known it once he arrived, fifteen minutes prior to showtime.

He exited his vehicle to enthusiastic applause, signed a few autographs and was met by Walt von Hauffe, the Castro's promotional director (who masterminded the screening with Allied Advertising's Shannon Valcich). When von Hauffe, a legend himself in the promotions game, introduced himself, Tarantino excitedly told him, "Thank you so much for doing this!"

The Oscar-winning director didn't sequester himself. He took his seat smack dab in the middle of the theater and chatted with the folks around him until he was introduced to the enthusiastic crowd. Just prior to the movie, he took the stage and waxed poetic about the nation's remaining stand-alone non-chain theaters.

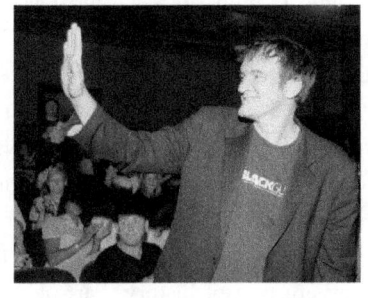

"Tonight is the very first time I've ever screened one of my movies in San Francisco with an audience and I'm thrilled it's at the Castro!" But after the kind words, he screamed, "Who wants to see some *Basterds*? Who wants to fuck up some Nazis?"

The crowd ate it up and appeared to love the film. All the riotous laughter and gasps were in the right places (the woman next to me reacted physically every time a Nazi was scalped, nudging me a few times. I almost offered her popcorn).

Once all the closing credits had unspooled, Tarantino took the stage and remained for nearly an hour, answering questions and running the room. Many stood up just to say what fans they were.

Others had scene-specific queries (yes, that was Harvey Keitel's voice as the General on the phone) or observations about his writing. Tarantino kept returning to the theme of starting new projects and facing the blank page, what he called "climbing the mountain."

Interestingly, Tarantino described his creative process as starting not with the story but the genre. In the case of *Basterds*, it was a "World War II genre pic," in particular, a "Guys on a mission pic." When asked what other genres he'd be interested in, he said "Well, I don't really see me doing a sci-fi movie, bunch of guys on a spaceship, not really my thing. But I could see myself doing a full-on, balls-out horror movie. I could do a western. Maybe it's been a while. I could throw my hat back in the crime film ring again."

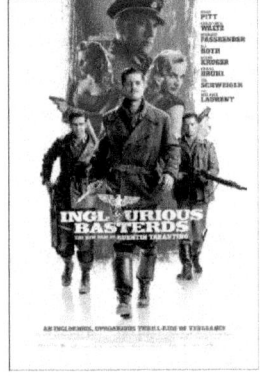

Basterds will certainly attract criticism for Tarantino's finale, which rewrites a significant amount of history. "Originally that wasn't the case, but then I thought, wait a minute! My characters don't know they are part of history. Part of the thing with my writing style with my characters is that there's nothing they can't do. I've never tried to play God. There aren't doors they can't walk through. And for me to step in there and act like God and steer them away from where they want to go, I've never done it before and now's not the time to start!"

When an audience member asked if *Basterds'* deliberate pacing and penchant for talk-over-action was his "message to Hollywood" to nudge movies back to a place where story was most important, he said "It would be nice if it worked out that way. That's just the way I write."

"Other countries did what they did (regarding contributions to film). What Hollywood did was that we told stories better than anyone else. But now, most movies are big versions of situation comedies: They set up the situation in the first fifteen minutes and the rest of the movie is living up to that situation. In a real story, you don't know everything there is to know the first fifteen minutes. A real story unfolds."

He admits that he's no longer interested in writing for others any more. "You see these writer-directors and they have two or three movies that have this voice. Then they start taking jobs, directing other people's scripts and after a while, they've made five, six, seven films but the voice is gone."

Thus far, his approach seems to be working. "I start off with a blank piece of paper and start from scratch. That's the way to keep it personal, that's the way to keep my voice, that's the way to keep it Quentin, for better or worse."

By the time Tarantino say his good-byes, it was hard not to feel like you'd spent time who was a master at his craft, a guy equally confident about his abilities and humble about his opportunities. "I am embarrassingly fortunate. *Kill Bill* was a dream project. *Pulp Fiction* was a dream project. I am in the position to, I'm almost embarrassed to say, to practice my art … so long as it doesn't cost too crazy much."

But he also knows his way around a stage and from the time he stepped out of that car – shaking hands, chatting with folks, posing for pictures, telling funny stories, cursing freely, dropping cinema-savvy nuggets the way most people talk about the weather – to the time he climbed back in, his stage was every inch of the Castro Theater.

He is Quentin Tarantino, after all, and goddamn well knows it.

CHRISTOPHER NOLAN

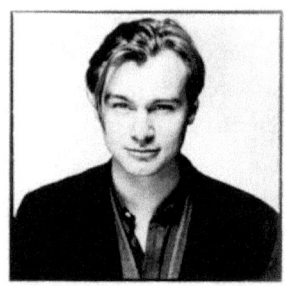

There are many filmmakers who make a splash with a clever low-budget film and get their shot to move into the Hollywood ranks. There are *not* many filmmakers who make it count, and even less that do so within the confines of an established comic book universe.

Christopher Nolan's second film *Memento* (2000) was a mind-bending thriller that unfolded backwards and was more of a whydunit than a whodunit. His follow-up *Insomnia* (2002) was a remake of a 1997 Norwegian film that starred Al Pacino and Robin Williams. It wasn't a runaway hit but it made money and was a well-regarded thriller.

When Nolan pitched Warner Brothers on an idea to revive the dormant *Batman* franchise, nobody was clamoring for a *Batman Begins*. But Nolan's version was a revelation, grounded in reality, fiercely violent, and more about Bruce Wayne, Batman's alter-ego, than the Caped Crusader.

The inevitable sequel was announced and it would feature The Joker, to be played by Heath Ledger, a dynamic young actor. It was also called *The Dark Knight,* thereby sending a message that this second film would indeed be something different and special.

Then in January 2008, just six months before the film was to be released, Heath Ledger was found dead in his apartment. It's hard to tell whether it was morbid fascination that drove the box office or the fact that the film was so well-received. It was a grand crime saga about how far you could bend a good man before he breaks; it became the third biggest domestic release ever and earned Ledger a posthumous Academy Award for his performance.

Of course, Warner Brothers wanted a sequel but there was something that Nolan wanted first: the opportunity to make his dream project (literally).

Inception became the poster child for supporting original ideas at the box office, and an argument for creativity over summer sequelitis.

What follows are my reviews for *Batman Begins* and *Inception*, the two big-budget films in which Nolan had something big on the line, something to lose. Not just studio money, but respect, mojo and to borrow from one of his titles, *prestige*.

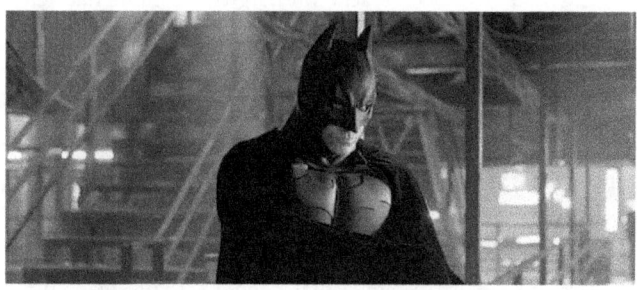

Batman Begins: Dirty Harry in a Cowl
June 15, 2005

Is there a more recently flawed and compromised series in recent Hollywood history than the 80's and 90's Batman films? As much as the Warner brass has tried the old "Hey, there were multiple James Bonds" argument, all you have to do is line the four DVD covers up and look at them side by side.

The rundown: nine super villains, two distinctly different directors, vastly differing costumes and worlds, and a rotating door of men in black tights, three in all.

And while it's easy to blame George Clooney and Arnold Schwarzenegger for the flamboyant failure that was 1997's *Batman and Robin*, truth be told it could have been anyone from Russell Crowe to the reanimated ghost of Lawrence Olivier underneath that cowl. They say that crème rises, but other things float too, and any attempt by the WB to throw promotional money to get people to watch or buy that last film was not unlike polishing one.

Blaming the fey sensibilities of second director Joel Schumacher is easy too. After all, it was his infamous Bat suits with fake nipples that sent fanboys up the bat pole in a tizzy (Funny, I wonder if the same ire would have been reached if Batgirl's costume had featured the same, ahem, accoutrements. But I digress.)

While I appreciate Tim Burton's place in the world as a gifted man-child wunderkind with a penchant for twisted fairy tales, I never felt that his two *Batman* movies were that great. His second, *Batman Returns*, was my favorite but that's like saying McDonald's processed chicken nuggets were better than Burger King's.

Boy, those boys at Warner Bros sure had their work cut out for them to create a Batman movie that people actually wanted to see. What the hell were the bean counters thinking when they began developing a Year One Batman movie after this lumpy, mismatched quadrilogy of campy freaks and garish colors? What was in the water at those creative meetings?

Whatever it was on the day somebody decided to hand the reins to writer-director Christopher Nolan was all too fleeting in an industry in which the people who design the video box have more power than the director in many cases. Christopher Nolan? The guy who directed *Memento*?

And then a strange thing happened: the impossible Batman movie that nobody wanted to see suddenly had buzz.

And for better or worse, Nolan's Batman flies in the face of all that have come before. It's dark, foreboding, creepy, insanely violent and realistic, in a way that is more practical than a summer superhero has a right or reason to be. The villains can't fly and don't speak in bad puns: One, Falcone (Tom Wilkinson), is a gangster, plain and simple. The other, The Scarecrow, has a few tricks up his sleeve but his mask is nothing more than protection from his own serum. The Batmobile works in a way that makes sense and even Gotham City, depicted in the other films with mile-high skyscrapers, looks as you would expect New York or Chicago to look. Forget Batman, this is Dirty Harry in a cowl.

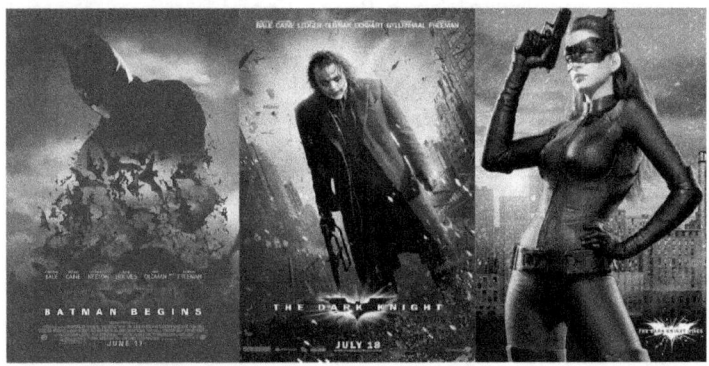

Unlike the superhero cool of Michael Keaton, Val Kilmer and George Clooney once they put on the mask, Christian Bale's Dark Knight is a feral, angry, immediate presence. He screams at drug dealers while interrogating them, his mouth curled into a snarl that can't hide his bubbling-over mania. He's crazy, but in a way that would make you feel good to have him on your side in a bar brawl. And when you consider that this is a billionaire who chooses to embrace an alter ego to fight crime and not some guy stuck with a power he doesn't want, well, that's the only way to play a guy like that. Bugnuts.

The title is misleading. Sure, this movie has Batman in it but the first thing writers David Goyer and Nolan get right is making it a Bruce Wayne movie first. And the masked crusader isn't Wayne's *only* alter ego. To hide the fact that all that cool gear may have come from his family's company, Wayne Enterprises, Bruce adopts a *second* personae -- that of the immature headline-grabbing billionaire playboy who shags debutantes and wantonly buys buildings because he can.

Bruce's two confidants are Lucius Fox (Morgan Freeman), Batman's equivalent of James Bond's Q and of course, devoted butler Alfred (Michael Caine), who is much more worldly and tough than his saintly demeanor may lead on. Katie Holmes is Rachel, a love interest that makes sense as a character given her childhood with Bruce, and I'm happy to report that after a wobbly first scene, acquits herself nicely as a worthy opponent.

Batman Begins has the best cast in recent memory with every role, major or minor, played by A-listers giving great performances. Even Gary Oldman, who I once trounced as the worst over-actor of the 90's, is subdued as the kind-hearted Lieutenant Gordon, a good cop in a sea of corruption.

Even if the powers that be had no idea what they were doing, they did something right when they greenlit this film. I hope we get Nolan's proposed trilogy and steer clear of any more campy super villains and advice from bean counters ("It has to be funnier! Focus Group A found this line of dialogue unlikable...").

Let's face it, Bale is the most interesting Batman to date, capable of being brutal and sympathetic at the same time; and Nolan and Goyer's vision represents the most stunning and impressive rebooting of a sagging franchise since Bond's *GoldenEye*.

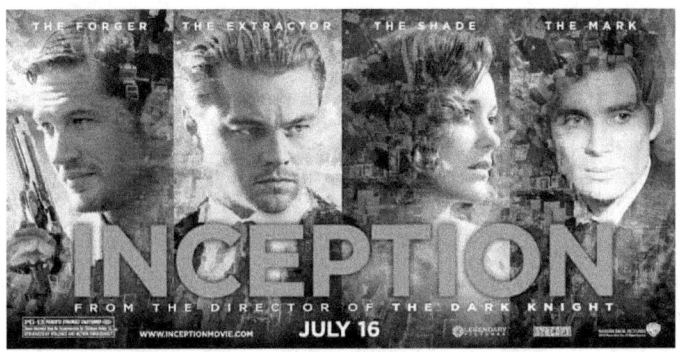

Inception: Running Down a Dream
July 23, 2010

There are dreamscapes and puzzles that go layers deep in Christopher Nolan's hotly-anticipated follow up to *The Dark Knight*.

It's a premise so fantastical that any Hollywood suit worth his Rolex would have demanded the very idea get whittled down to one sentence so it could fit on the poster. But when you've just directed the Oscar-winning third-biggest film ever released, you can get away with aiming a little higher. Why play checkers when you can bust out Mr. Spock's three-dimensional chess set instead?

Inception is the story of thieves who can break into your mind and steal your ideas while you dream. Now add the concept of shared dreams and what each person brings to the scenario, their insecurities, fears, guilt, regrets – right down to how quickly the subconscious forms ideas.

It's also about dreams within dreams, planting ideas and hiding things you could never share. Imagine *Eternal Sunshine of the Spotless Mind* as a $150 million heist flick. Like that 2004 mind-bender, the technology is never explained. But there are rules: to be followed, to be broken, and a few that have been left off the table for discovery later.

Rare is the film that can provide that fizzy sense of newness and discovery, and for that, Nolan must be praised. He also gets points for creating a dense dream landscape that never breaks internal continuity or becomes impenetrable.

Leonardo DiCaprio plays Dom Cobb, the leader of an underground team skilled in stealing thoughts. He's wanted for a crime he didn't commit, desperately misses his children and agrees to a risky and rare job – to plant an idea – as a means to get home. He's haunted by dreams of his deceased wife, Mal (Marion Cotillard), who shows up at the most inopportune times, usually in the middle of a sensitive shared dream. Because she's really Dom's projection of his own guilt, Mal functions as the movie's de facto villain, both a dream-level terminator and the emotion driving him.

Enter Ellen Page, the whip-smart "architect," who figures out early on that Cobb hasn't exactly laid all his cards on the table to his team. She acts as his right hand gal, guiding him (and us) through his messy emotions and the labyrinthine plot, which has to do with planting an idea and making the subject think they came up with it – but to do that, the team will have to go deep and manipulate the mark's equally messy relationship with his industrialist father.

The cast is superb: aside from indie darlings Page and Gordon-Levitt, there's Watanabe as the client, Murphy as the mark, and Hardy (fresh off the amazing Bronson and bound for a pair of Mad Max movies). Nolan also makes limited but crucial use of Tom Berenger, Lukas Haas, Pete Postlethwaite and his good-luck charm Michael Caine.

It's nearly impossible to discuss the progression of the story without spoilers, so I'll limit it to this. If you die in a dream, you simply wake up. So, where is the suspense? Well, because of the variables on that rule and a very clever point-of-no-return at the halfway point. It also never hurts to have a ticking clock and this film has a doozie.

DiCaprio plays a similar role in his Martin Scorsese thriller *Shutter Island* in that off-screen events regarding the fate of his wife have put him in the situation he's in – and that the revelation is a key moment in the film. But the Scorsese movie falls down on the ultimate reveal, ham-fisting and over-explaining it.

It's Nolan's technical proficiency that turns this into an instant classic. Inception is a slam-bang action flick with expert choreography and a perfect balance between real stunts and CGI. It's a heist flick with twists, reversals and improbable obstacles. It's a mind-blowing, physics-bending fantasy that manages to unfold simultaneously on four different levels of the subconscious.

And if it was just one of those things, it would be worthy of an audience's attention. I'm also very pleased to report that the trailers give nothing away, even the most recent one that's loaded with expository dialogue.

Nolan's use of visual trickery and sound to convey emotion and tension would have made Hitchcock proud. And he manages to deliver an original must-see visual big-screen event devoid of marketing spoilers or tacky added-value 3D in a summer filled with remakes and sequels.

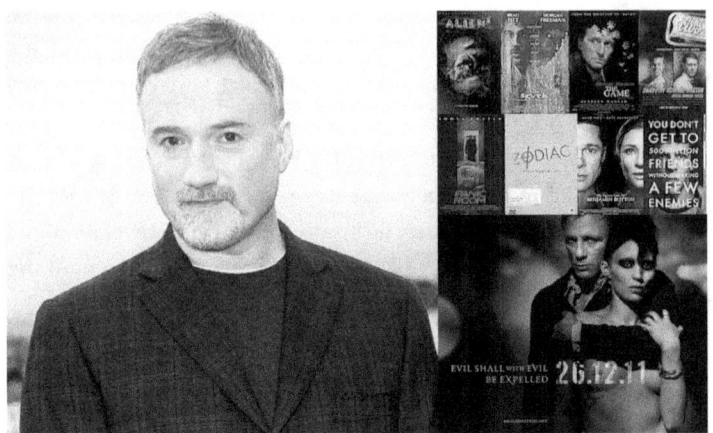

DAVID FINCHER

There is no ballsier filmmaker working within the studio system than David Fincher. He killed off Sigourney Weaver in *Alien 3*. He allowed the bad guy to win in *Se7en*. And he dared to end *The Game* as if it were *The Wizard Of Oz* with Michael Douglas saying "...and you were there..."

He built an entire movie around an unsolved crime spree (*Zodiac*), shot the American version of a beloved Swedish film (*The Girl with the Dragon Tattoo*), turned a movie about Facebook into a breathtakingly human tale, and created *Fight Club*, one of the most prescient and blistering statements ever issued by a major studio.

His technical proficiency and predilection for controlling every pixel of every frame is legendary. Actors sign onto his films knowing their days will be filled doing as many as 100 takes on something as simple as walking through a door. But they will also likely be appearing in a future classic.

If David Fincher had never made the leap to the big screen, his iconic status would have been intact as the director of striking (and classic) music videos from Madonna ("Express Yourself," "Vogue," "Oh Father"), Billy Idol ("Cradle of Love"), Paula Abdul ("Straight Up," "Cold Hearted"), Aerosmith ("Janie's Got a Gun"), Rolling Stones ("Love Is Strong"), Don Henley ("The End of the Innocence"), "Roy Orbison ("She's a Mystery to Me"), George Michael ("Freedom '90"), Michael Jackson ("Who Is It"), and many, many more.

Fincher's first theatrical film, *Alien 3* (1992) was famously taken away and re-edited. Thankfully, his director's cut exists and it's a vast improvement. His follow-up, *Se7en* (1995) wasn't just a serial killer flick, it became *the* serial killer flick.

Se7en was filled with gruesome imagery, but it's the emotional jolts that resonate years later. And what an ending!

But in considering the resume of David Fincher, there are two films, unlikely bookends, which best define the director's ability to tap the societal vein of what simmers beneath the surface of a culture.

Fight Club (1999) is the response to corporate consumerism and apathy, using ultra-violence as a metaphor for the uneasy reflection of a country grappling with the uncertainties of a looming new century. And what an ending!

One decade later, *The Social Network* (2010) depicted the early days of Facebook, the internet platform that redefined the way people communicate. This film captured the pulse of an era filled with possibility, with technology as an ally.

One is about destruction, the other creation. One is a caustic tale with a twist ending; the other is a vibrant reminder that all the gadgets in the world can't bring happiness.

In both cases, it's the basic need to connect with one another pushing our protagonists to take personal leaps that have lasting reverberations throughout the society at large.

Fight Club: Gentlemen, Start Your Vengeance

October 20, 1999

Fight Club may appear on its surface exactly what it sounds like: the story of two guys who start an after-hours bare-knuckle boxing club. But percolating below this film's kinetic surface is an anarchy that suggests a fascist uprising is the only salvation against the evils of brand names and corporate coffee houses.

In the wrong hands, it could be a dangerous message. But then again, as the film tells us, the basic ingredients in a bar of soap could be dangerous in the hands of someone intent on building bombs.

Our narrator is Jack (Edward Norton), an insomniac who gets himself addicted to support groups in an effort to restore a form of normalcy to his mundane existence. The groups allow him to anonymously cry like a baby, and expel all of his pent-up frustration from a crappy job assessing automobile accidents and how they might affect possible recalls.

This is, until he meets Marla (Helena Bonham Carter), a cynical spitfire who, herself, has become a support group tourist. Marla's own dishonesty unmasks his, and she becomes the representation of all that disgusts him.

On a plane flight from an accident scene, he meets Tyler Durden (Brad Pitt), a scummy soap manufacturer who lives in the moment. From their very first exchange, we get the impression Tyler is the aggressive voice Jack has been craving all along. Tyler's brutal honesty frees Jack from the shackles of pretending he's got cancer, an eating disorder, or is even content at his job. And then Tyler gets to his point: *I want you to hit me as hard as you can.*

Whoa. The boys figure that there's no better way to live in the moment then beating each other to a bloody pulp, and to a certain degree, they're right. Fight Club is born, and soon, Jack and Tyler have legions of followers gathering on Saturday nights to take each other on--two at a time--and free from their daytime identities.

Rule one of Fight Club is that you don't talk about Fight Club. Rule two is the same.

Of course, Marla returns, and when she does, it's in the bed of Tyler, which doesn't sit well with Jack. Read what you will into the conflict: homoerotic tension ... love triangle ... but at one point, her presence becomes very clear. She serves as the engine for the film's (and the novel's) kookiest turn.

Just as the first McDonalds or Starbucks caught on and became a chain, Fight Clubs begin springing up all over the country. Jim Uhls' vibrant adaptation of Chuck Palahniuk's novel warns us about the evils of crass consumerism, and serves up this perfect, albeit violent parable.

Fight Club isn't just about fighting; it's about mayhem against corporate America. In one of the movie's sharpest observations, Jack tells us that from here on in, any deep space exploration would

result in consumer-based brand names for new galaxies.

Fincher's visual style is eclectic, to be sure. His camera will show us an entire room in one shot and take us through somebody's pores in the next. At times, the characters have their thoughts displayed visually for us. Other times, they break the fourth wall and talk to us directly. It's a film with a different agenda, so it makes perfect sense to march to its own rhythm.

Like Oliver Stone's *Natural Born Killers*, Mr. Fincher's opus is bound only by its own cinematic rules, and the experience is a visceral one.

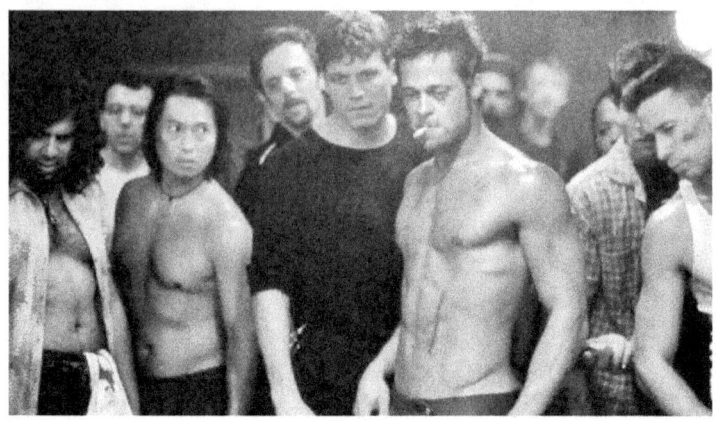

The performances are all rock solid. Brad Pitt is as good here as he was in *12 Monkeys* or *Se7en* (his other Fincher collaboration), all chiseled and id. Edward Norton adds another impressive turn with a very complicated performance (many other critics have spoiled the biggest revelation, but I wouldn't dream of it).

As the simultaneous narrator, tour guide and voice of reason, Norton proves once again his ability to seek out and deliver finite performances. Helena Bonham Carter casts aside her Merchant-Ivory corset for the rags of a loveable scumbag.

And believe it or not, Meat Loaf Aday (yep, the same one, now sporting his last name) is tender, tragic and funny in a truly weird character turn as a testicular amputee with extremely large female breasts. Go ahead and read that last sentence again, but I'll tell you now. You read it correctly the first time.

It would be a sad and fitting tribute to this bleak vision if Fight Clubs did spring up. As hyper-realistic as it all may sound, the film really is one big, angry guffaw. It dares the audience to look into this truly wretched mirror of our perceived mediocrity and to rise up. And then, it laughs at the absurdity of it all. The final shot is as ludicrous and potent as Slim Pickens riding the bomb like a bronco in *Dr. Strangelove.*

Advocacy groups will point to this film next time a high school kid senselessly beats the hell out of another, but I guess that's better than shooting each other. Also, I hope the finger-pointers (and the wayward wannabes) take note: violence does have horrible conclusions in this film. Faces swell up, teeth get punched out, and bones are broken.

But what good would it do if we started beating the crap out of each other, anyway? There are far healthier ways to shake off the bindings of our mundane existences.

Like, say, writing movie reviews.

The Social Network: The Movie of the Decade

October 1, 2010

Mark Zuckerberg, as performed by Jesse Eisenberg, is painfully inept at the most basic human interaction and yet would go on to invent Facebook, the most popular and vast social network ever devised.

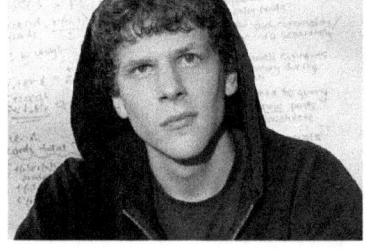

This dichotomy is one of the many ironies that power David Fincher's fast-paced and chatty movie that was promoted as being as relevant to the '00s as *Easy Rider* was to the '60s. I can see that. Any film that can create a universally-felt sense of anticipation from the simple act of adding someone as a Facebook friend has obviously tapped into a paradigm shift.

As we open, Zuckerberg, then a 20-year-old Harvard geek, is having drinks with his girlfriend (Mara, famously cast in the remake of *The Girl with the Dragon Tattoo*). As the scene progresses, we learn Zuckerberg is obsessed with exclusive clubs and bitter he'll never be invited to join one.

He doesn't possess much of a filter and ends up insulting her over and over, not that he could help himself or really even know the difference. She breaks up with him, reminding him that it's not because he's a geek, but an A-hole, something he'll deal with his whole life.

So, he gets drunk and blogs disparagingly about her. But he also simultaneously hacks into college databases to access their "face books" and creates an instant online sensation called Facemash. The kid might not know how to talk to girls but he can whip up an online sensation the way others make breakfast.

He quickly attracts the attention of Cameron and Tyler Winklevoss (Hammer), Harvard twins that act as two parts of the same whole, like a gentlemanly version of Master Blaster (*Mad Max: Beyond Thunderdome*). They contact Zuckerberg about creating a Harvard-based social network that would be special because of its exclusivity. Zuckerberg keeps the "Winklevii" at bay, and then goes in a different direction, coding a preliminary version of Facebook that would be special because anyone could join.

That's one of the two lawsuits that provide the structure of the movie as both cases progress in concurrent depositions. Facts emerge and conflict, telling a story that comes together as the puzzle pieces reveal themselves. But the movie isn't leading toward a big revelation. Its strengths are the pieces as characters are eventually built and an incredible world is slowly uncovered.

As interpreted by the lively pen of *The West Wing's* Sorkin, it's loaded with memorable scene-stealing characters and crackling dialogue. But it's not content to be a paint-by-numbers biopic with archetypes. Here, the Harvard jocks are gentlemen first and the hackers are the party animals. The movie never judges any of its characters, even when they do horrible things to each other.

Eisenberg pulls off a very difficult trick of creating an antagonist/anti-hero that's both likable and an insufferable prick. When he makes bad personal decisions (that would eventually make him a lot of money) and his friends start dropping like flies, he becomes the poster child for 21st century youthful ambition. And his expression barely changes.

Timberlake plays Sean Parker (Napster's co-founder) with blinding confidence and cockiness, just the right amount of fireworks to distract Zuckerberg from the fact that he has a wicked competitive streak. Garfield is Zuckerberg's best friend Eduardo Saverin and it's hard not to feel bad for him once the sinewy Parker starts making his play. One actor (Hammer) plays both Winklevoss twins (with another credited actor standing in as a body double), but you'd never know it.

Fincher's technical team gets the little things so right that they never distract. For once, the sound of music in a club or a bar seems

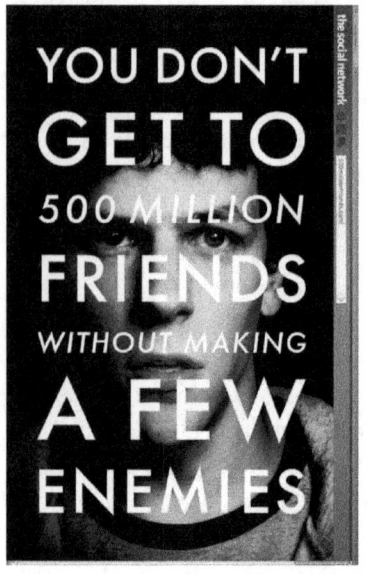

just about right and computers don't make fake bleepy sounds for cinematic effect. In all fairness, most of the movie's charms reveal themselves not during the initial viewing but when playing it all back in your head afterward.

To say *The Social Network* is greater than the sum of its parts is only part of the story, which is why the movie continues to resonate and vibrate long after it's done. It comments on a particular time, acting as a snapshot.

It asks (but never answers) questions about such varied ideas as content ownership and friends both real and virtual. It holds a mirror up to a plugged-in generation and dares to treat the technology as a side dish, as if to remind us that they way we treat each other is more powerful than any widget, however enticing.

POSTSCRIPT:

The Social Network swept 2010 award season, landing on over 50 Top Ten lists. It was named Best Picture by over 30 critics' groups, as well as the National Board of review and the Golden Globes (Drama). Alas, despite all that acclaim, the Academy Awards for Best Picture and Best Director went to *The King's Speech* in one of the most lopsided finales in award history.

8 FOR YOUR CONSIDERATION

(PUT THESE MOVIES IN YOUR QUEUE, NOW!)

Okay, let's have some fun!

I sure complain a lot, but it's only because I love cinema, and get frustrated at how great ideas get hobbled by runaway egos, poor marketing and asinine decisions at the studio level.

But I'm just like most people in that when the movie starts, I want to have the best time possible. I've said it before: make me laugh, piss me off, turn me on, make me think, or wow me with whooshy 3D effects. Just don't bore me.

But let's face it, what we *think* we *should* like isn't often in line with what we *do* like. How many Netflix queues are filled with esoteric classics, while we're watching repeats of *Married With Children* or *Caddyshack*? Guilty as charged.

This next section is a series of reviews of films that I adored. Some are high-brow, many are not. But in most cases, they are films that have either fallen off the pop culture radar or simply need to be discovered for the first time.

Included are films from Ben Affleck (the director), brilliant social critics Mike Judge and Trey Parker & Matt Stone, who also happen to make bold, funny films. And it's criminal how many people don't know about *Paul*, the satire from Simon Pegg, Nick Front and Greg Mottola (*Adventureland*) that takes on everything from classic sci-fi to religion.

Watch these movies and tell me what you think at dennis@denniswillis.net. If you have any favorite movies, I'd love to hear about them!

Drive

September 15, 2011

Ryan Gosling is a Hollywood stunt driver by day and getaway driver by night. He doesn't speak much, nobody calls him by name and his existence is a spartan one.

The Driver is a cipher, a blank slate that hides, one presumes, a former life that led him here: Los Angeles, working in an auto shop

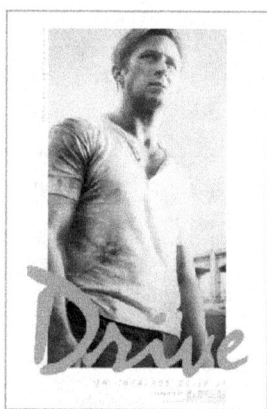

for kindly Shannon (Bryan Cranston), a guy who has made one too many bad deals with the wrong types of people and walks with a permanent limp because of it.

One day, the driver meets his comely neighbor, Irene (Carey Mulligan), and her wise-beyond-his-years son. Turns out the kid's dad is in jail, and is getting out soon. But what of the burgeoning relationship forming between her and the driver?

I would never dream of spoiling this contemporary LA noir flick but I'll elaborate on a few things worth mentioning, such as the inspired casting. Who knew Albert Brooks had it in him to be this imposing and lethal? He's well-paired with Ron Perlman, who plays a "west coast" goombah with something to prove.

Nicholas Winding Refn also directed the Kubrick-esque tour-de-force *Bronson* (2009), a movie that featured a hellzapoppin' performance from Tom Hardy. For his follow up, Refn seems to be channeling 1980s-era Michael Mann, in particular, *Manhunter* (1986), and steers Gosling through this human maze of destruction with as much minimalism as Bronson was flashy.

Layering his beautifully-composed widescreen visuals with sheets of moody synthesizers is a stunning directorial choice, not the first time we've seen this technique, but it's been a while since anyone has used it this effectively.

The opening sequence, which takes place in the aftermath of a heist, is a master class in editing and timing. And although some critics (and audience) have taken exception with Refn's use of deliberate (slow) pacing, tension-inducing electro-pop soundtrack and explosive violence, I think the combination is hypnotic, if not damn near perfect.

What most directors don't understand is that without coil, there is no satisfaction in the release. *Drive* slowly builds to the point of measured hysteria just under the surface. When Gosling walks into a strip club dressing room and tightens his grip on a hammer, it's more explosive than a hailstorm of bullets.

We get all the information needed in the margins and what's not explicitly stated grows in our minds and fills in the blanks. Refn won the Best Director award at the 2011 Cannes Film Festival, but the movie received little traction when released wide.

That's probably just as well. If it was a huge hit, Hollywood studios would churn out an assembly line of slick, moody copycats but likely miss the point entirely.

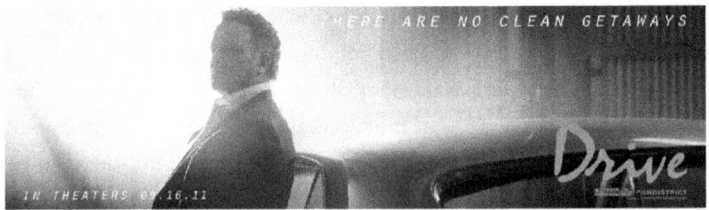

Gone Baby Gone

October 19, 2007

Gone Baby Gone is such a relevant, infuriating, breathtaking piece of cinema, it's very easy to forget what a punchline its director and co-writer Ben Affleck had become. This two hours all but erases the doubt about whether Affleck and Matt Damon actually wrote *Good Will Hunting* (rumors to the contrary have dogged the due since the Oscar win), all of Ben's paycheck grabs as an actor, and hell - possibly even the phenomenon known as Bennifer.

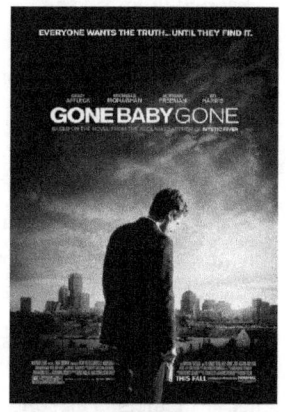

Yeah, it's that good.

There were a million ways to screw up adapting *Gone Baby Gone*, the fourth in a series built around Boston detectives and lovers Patrick Kenzie (Casey Affleck) and Angie Gennero (Michelle Monaghan). Dennis Lehane's novel about the kidnapping of a four-year old girl from one of the worst neighborhoods in Boston is a demanding piece with a murky morality, offering arguments for and against, but never really taking a stand either way.

In doing so, Affleck has guaranteed the movie will have a life of its own. I cannot imagine anybody with an IQ higher than a pencil not wanting to weigh in on the last act, which poses an infuriating argument so compelling that it's discovery (as a viewer or reader) reveals why this project exists in the first place.

The question posed is the meat of the whole thing - but in deference those who are not familiar with the story, such spoilery conversations will have to be left up to you.

If Affleck the director had merely serviced this powerful tale, it would still be one of the best films of 2007. But by choosing atmosphere over tired movie beats, he creates a dangerous world befitting of these colorful characters. This is Dorchester, a neighborhood where the roughest customers would be best advised to keep to themselves.

As we open, Helene McCredie (Amy Ryan) is weathering a media storm over the disappearance of her daughter. And what a piece of work she is - drug addicted, profane, dumb as a post - and it only gets worse as the stories start coming out.

The innocent girl didn't ask to be kidnapped, but she also didn't ask for this cretin of a mother. Ryan devours this role with relish. It's the kind of blinding star-making moment that can build career momentum for a long time.

Almost every character is cast note perfect: Morgan Freeman takes a complex role worthy of his talent after too many paychecks gigs; Ed Harris is as solid as usual (why does this man not have an Oscar?); and damn, it was good seeing Amy Madigan and John Ashton again.

Casey Affleck probably knew he would have to fend off cries of nepotism, so he transforms himself once again. After such a nebbishy turn in *The Assassination of Jesse James by the Coward Robert Ford*, it's quite surprising to see Affleck play such a flawed, but interesting character. He's slight and pretty, but acts tough and acquits himself well against random bursts of barroom violence.

Of the entire ensemble, only Michelle Monaghan seemed a little lost. As Angie, half the investigating team, she doesn't get much to do, but when it absolutely counts, she's there to rip your heart out.

And that's why *Gone Baby Gone* is such an exciting entry in the tired suspense genre. At the midpoint, the movie switches gears and heads down a different path with a new set of circumstances and choices, perfectly setting up the real theme: that the choices we make have long-term effects.

It very simply asks us all to consider if we could live with ourselves under the same circumstances. It's that question which haunts us long after the film has finished.

Idiocracy

September 30, 2006

As legend goes, Mike Judge ran afoul of the powers that be at Twentieth Century Fox. The result was the banishing of his second live action comedy *Idiocracy* to a handful of theatres with no trailers, no ads, no poster and no press screenings, before an unceremonious dump to video.

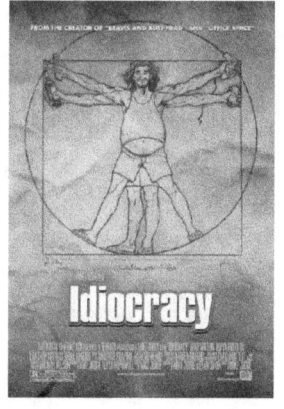

The official line was that test audiences did not understand the movie. Um, this is a movie about how stupid we are becoming and the focus groups aren't smart enough to understand that?

Why, that kinda sounds like the kind of thing Mike Judge was satirizing in the first place.

Idiocracy is a comedic take on *Buck Rogers in the 25th Century*, but with dumb-asses instead of Draconians. In the 21st century, a very ordinary man named Joe (Luke Wilson) is recruited to become the first cryogenically frozen man, but instead of staying asleep for a year, he wakes up in 2505, where the IQ has dropped so much, he is now the smartest man on the planet.

People in the future speak in grunts, sponsored catch-phrases, homie and redneck slang, and think anybody who reads or speaks in full sentences is "faggy." They go to movie theaters to watch movies like *Ass* (which is 90 minutes of a naked butt, farting) and watch shows like *Ow, My Balls*, which has a man getting repeatedly bashed in the clackers.

After a hilarious introduction comparing a "smart" couple who puts off having kids and the "stupid" couple who spawn redneck rugrats at a furious pace (which of course, paves the way for the devolution of the world), Judge continues a social observation he began 15 years earlier with *Beavis and Butt-head*.

He also focuses his satirical laser on corporations. In the future, people can go to college at city-sized Costcos and a large corporation will eventually buy the FDA and replace water with a Gatorade-like substance manufactured by the biggest corporation in the world. People repeat things like "It has electrolytes" and "the taste plants crave" because they have been programmed to.

500 years? Sounds like that's what happening now!

You can get handjobs at Starbuck and you don't even want to know what Fuddruckers will be called (for my money, I'd love to know what it took to convince the Fuddruckers board to sign off on *that* little bit of product placement).

Wilson and Maya Rudolph (as a 21st century prostitute) are good and the movie is fall-down funny more times than not. In fact, never at any time does the joke get old because the story has forward momentum (something about the quest for a time machine to get back home). Sure, it's been done before and really doesn't say anything new. But Mike Judge is America's premiere social critic and just happens to be a really funny guy.

Under normal circumstances, given a reasonable theatrical release pattern, I would have expected *Idiocracy* to become as big a hit as, say, *Beerfest*.

But *Idiocracy* is now the missed opportunity of 2006, thanks to the think tank at Fox that felt *Garfield: A Tale Of Two Kitties* and *Date Movie* were better matches for their audiences' IQs.

Now, that's idiocracy.

Paul

March 18, 2011

Look no further than the pedigree of this film for everything you need to know: Simon Pegg co-wrote both *Shaun of the Dead* and *Hot Fuzz* (2007), two satires that so perfectly mocked their genres (zombies, buddy cop flicks) that they stand not just as parodies but almost as the last word on those genres.

With *Paul*, you can check off anything having to do with UFOs,

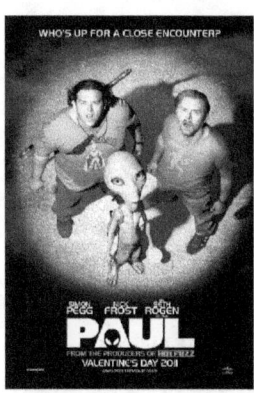

Spielbergian sci-fi flicks and geek culture in general. This movie has it all. And yet *Paul* isn't just a series of random jokes. Pardon the comparison but if you were an alien from space, you might just take one look at *Paul* and mistake it for the real deal.

British comic book nerds Graeme Willy (Pegg) and Clive Gollings (Nick Frost) attend ComicCon in San Diego before making their way in a rented RV to visit the sites of America's most celebrated UFO landmarks. They run afoul of local thugs and while escaping, encounter Paul, a cigar-smoking alien who's been hanging around Earth since crashing in 1947 (turns out he's not a very good driver).

Paul is very Americanized and sounds like, well, like Seth Rogen, who invests more into this voiceover than he did in his attempt to play the Green Hornet. The reason he looks like the stereotypical alien with big eyes and a slit for a mouth is because all alien imagery since Roswell has been derived from his appearance.

He's helped out the government, informed movies (a hysterical bit involves an actual Spielberg cameo) and even shared alien technology. But now, with nothing more to glean from him, Paul is on the run with agents are in hot pursuit, ordered by "The Big Guy," (Sigourney Weaver) to kill the alien.

Graeme and Clive pick up one-eyed Ruth (Kristen Wiig), a devout Christian whose beliefs last only until Paul mind-melds with her and shows her billions of years of evolution. She soon takes to cursing (not very well) and "planning to fornicate." But the gentle pokes at Christianity are hardly the point.

Paul has so many references to the classic sci-fi movies of the '70s and '80s that it takes several viewings to catch them all. Some are obvious: when Blythe Danner says "Get away from her, you bitch," it's a funny and obvious reference to Weaver in *Aliens*; ditto for when sunglasses-wearing agent Bateman shoots his own radio and says "Boring conversation anyway."

If you don't get that last reference, this movie might not be for you. Pegg and Frost nail the material but director Greg Mottola gets credit for reproducing the widescreen gravitas of those Spielberg flicks. And yes, Paul might be a CGI creation but he's completely believable as a character - and not just a wisecracking punch line that swears and sounds like Seth Rogen.

When the gang arrives at its final destination (which I won't ruin for you), the sequence is shot with all the verisimilitude of the finales of *Close Encounters of the Third Kind* (1977) or *E.T.* (1982), albeit with a few winks.

Pegg and Frost described this movie as a love letter to Spielberg, but it works well as the real deal too.

Team America: World Police
October 11, 2004

The 90's saw the rise of uber-producer Jerry Bruckheimer who gave us one simple-minded opus after another, building careers for hyperkinetic hacks. It didn't matter if the director was Dominic Sena (*Gone in 60 Seconds*), Tony Scott (*Crimson Tide, Enemy of the State*), or Michael Bay *(Armageddon, Pearl Harbor)* - any action movie made by one of Jerry's kids all looked and sounded exactly the same.

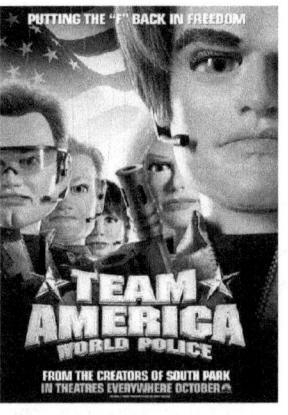

Team America: World Police has many agendas but topping the list seems to be how preposterous action films have become. In fact, there's an entire song that seems built around the idea that *Pearl Harbor* sucked, and asks why Bay gets to keep making movies.

Now that's a political argument I can get behind.

It becomes clear that Trey Parker and Matt Stone also really hate actors, perhaps even more than Dubya hates terrorists. *Team America: World Police* may seem to be yet another Hollywood-fanned polemic against the powers that be but falls very much in line with what the guys do each week on *South Park,* namely skewering every form of celebrity imaginable.

Politically, both the right and the left take it in the shorts here with the biggest guns reserved for those with the biggest pretensions. If you're an actor or a public figure and you have a loud opinion, Parker and Stone make it clear what they think of you. In short, shut the hell up and just "do acting."

The plot, which rivals the complexity of *Rambo III*, concerns a Broadway actor who masquerades as a terrorist to infiltrate a cell bent on world domination. After all, it's pointed out, spying is just like acting.

Sean Penn, Tim Robbins, Susan Sarandon, George Clooney and Danny Glover all appear as a coalition of actors rising to combat rampant American military violence, not realizing they are all pawns in Kim Jong Il's plan to destroy the world. They form the "Film Actors Guild" and I'll let you figure out the acronym. So far, only Penn has responded with a hearty F-bomb of his own, but I think it's fair to say that Parker and Stone won't make many Christmas card lists.

And just as it would have been as lacerating to set the same audio track to animated cardboard cut-outs ala *South Park*, Parker and Stone chose the art form of puppetry to express themselves. *Team America* may go down in history as the only marionette action movie that will ever be made and, as such, delivers enough ground-level camera swoops, corny montages and slow-motion explosions to make Jerry proud.

You've heard the term "equally opportunity offenders." Well, Trey and Matt could have business cards printed with that credit emblazoned proudly in bold letters. Nothing is sacred, from racial profiling to the global viewpoint that America polices the world. Not even 9/11. At one point, the team is told of an impending threat by saying it would be "9/11 times a hundred." Of course, someone replies, "Why, that would be 91,100!" It's that kind of movie.

References to other films come fast and frequently. The bar in Cairo teeming with terrorists features a band playing what sounds very much like the cantina song from *Star Wars*. A montage set to a song called "Montage" deconstructs that tired movie convention while pointing out that "even *Rocky* had a montage."

And then there's the macho patriotic posturing of "America (Fuck Yeah!)" which not only sounds like it came from *Top Gun*, but will never grace the stage at the Academy Awards. Neither will "I'm So Ronery," which is sung by Kim Jong Il in broken English like a Travolta ballad from *Grease*.

A sequence that shows a mournful puppet in real-world settings around Washington D.C. is one of the funniest gags in the film, proving the boys are so willing to satirize the entire entertainment industry; they even take the piss out of themselves.

Remarkably, there were no CG effects. Every single action shot, from car chases to rampaging waters to explosions and thunderous vomit (don't ask) all happen as practical effects on real sets, all scaled to the puppets, which are all about two feet tall. This is a colossal achievement once you factor in all the running, dancing, karate moves and fornication on display.

Notoriously, *Team America* tried *ten times* to land an R-rating from the MPAA because of a sex scene between the two lead puppets. Think about that for just a moment. Two non-anatomically correct wood puppets having sex. It sounds a bit ridiculous until you see the scene, which is jaw-droppingly, um, animated.

Of course, the MPAA didn't have a problem with puppets having their heads blown bloody wide open but there go our sensible American values again.

Once

March 23, 2007

In the 21st century, when you say "musical," it's easy to think of the bombast of *Moulin Rouge* or the episodic set pieces of *Chicago*. Usually there is choreography and most times people spontaneously burst into song for no apparent reason. Most musicals are fantasies, existing in alternate universes where such behavior is the norm.

Once is not one of those musicals.

Made for just $150,000 with long indie-style takes, real singing and a minimalist approach, *Once* tells a very simple story of a busker who meets his soul mate on the streets of Dublin and the week that follows.

The song lyrics say everything the characters will not or cannot say to each other, and the most revealing exchange of dialogue is spoken in Czech with no subtitles (thank heavens for the internet).

At first glance, it seems like it would be similar to the bloated Hugh Grant-Drew Barrymore yuck-fest *Music and Lyrics*. But *Once* is as refreshingly original as *Lyrics* seems shat from the McMovie assembly line.

We really want this couple (named only Guy and Girl) to get together and understand why they cannot. There are no music cues to tell us how to feel, no Hugh Grant finale with a declaration of love and nowhere does a secondary character (who exist only for such reasons in Hollywood films) spell out the obvious to our clueless leads.

Once is written and directed by John Carney, a former member of the Irish band The Frames and the Guy is played by The Frames' founder Glen Hansard (also one of the guitarists in Alan Parker's *The Commitments*). Since so much of the film deals with the unspoken process of creating art, the pedigree is not surprising. And now Hansard has appeared in the two best Dublin-based musicals!

What *is* entirely surprising is that the Girl -- Markéta Irglová - had never acted before appearing in this film. And yet, she is so serene, so commanding and so genuine (not to mention a great singer), she creates one of the most indelible characters of the year.

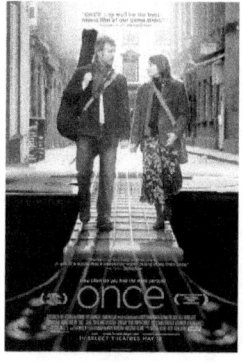

The ending is sublime. Make time to watch the last seven minutes twice, because much of the off-camera goodness might not be as apparent.

And while we're talking about sequences worth repeating, there is a long scene in a music shop at a piano that is one of the most dazzlingly human moments I've seen in years.

The song, "Falling Slowly," a delicate and joyous declaration of love, plays like all the stages of a first date with the Guy (on guitar) talking the Girl (on piano) through the changes in the song.

It is this scene, with its stolen glances and passion, that simultaneously captures the harmonious moment in which all instruments gloriously combine to make one sound, and makes it analogous to the fragility of falling in love. It's an instant classic scene and the heart of the movie.

Once is a great date movie. It is also a great independent film, and a great musical. You want it to continue so you can spend more time with these people and when it's all said and done, you want to turn around and watch it again. It's no surprise that audiences everywhere have carried this precious little film through a very long theatrical run.

It would not surprise me in the slightest if a Hollywood studio wanted to remake the film with more mainstream stars. And if they did, I'm sure it would look and feel exactly like *Music and Lyrics*...

POSTSCRIPT:

Once never became remade as a Hollywood movie but it did become a popular Broadway play, and nabbed a handful of Tony nominations. This is following the surprising Oscar win for "Falling Slowly," and the documentary *The Swell Season*, which depicted the fallout from Markéta Irglová and Glen Hansard's sudden stardom. It's a fascinating epilogue to this beloved tale, and I've included my review here:

The Swell Season

November 15, 2011

There are few Hollywood success stories as endearing and engaging as the tale of Glen Hansard and Markéta Irglová, the cutie pies who

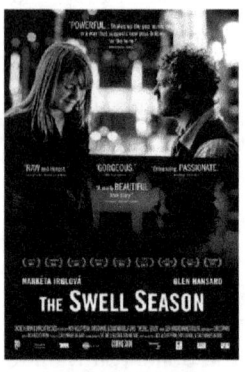

starred in the delightful indie musical *Once* (2007). As legend goes, they fell in love before our eyes while making music, then a year later, won the Academy Award for their stirring ballad "Falling Slowly."

But not every fairy tale ends with the words "happily ever after," and despite an introduction that reminds us of where their magical journey began, the tone quickly shifts as we follow the duo for the next few months through a world tour. Soon, the delicate touches and grand gestures give way to complacency and a fracturing of ideals.

Glen, the Irish wailer, understands that art requires a certain amount of commerce for it to actually reach people. For Markéta, the Czech pianist twenty years his junior, art is a pure expression and not all this celebrity-worshipping garbage.

In Hollywood, image is everything, an idea that runs counter to the organic ideals that brought them together in the first place. We live in a tabloid culture in which the marriages and breakups of celebrities are tracked like baseball statistics.

We've all heard stories about ungrateful celebrities when cornered for an autograph or when a fan feels a little too comfortable with somebody because they watch them on TV.

So how fascinating is it to gaze out of that fish bowl through their eyes, two people who just want to make music and get to know each other. It's equally fascinating and tragic watching them deal with the concept of stardom while trying to navigate their own creative and intimate lives.

The Swell Season not only documents the long fade out of a relationship, but reveals the deep emotional cracks in a person's psyche that causes them to want to create passionate music in the first place. In the end, we are still in love with Glen and Markéta, but no longer believe in the fairy tale.

8 Mile

November 15, 2002

Saturday Night Fever was the seminal music film of the 1970's because it captured a youth culture in the throes of an underground movement that could either flicker and die or explode.

Thanks to the star-power of John Travolta and a smash hit soundtrack, *Fever* took all things disco out of the nightclubs and launched a mainstream event. Twenty-five years later, it remains a vital snapshot of the late 70's, and, surprise, a good movie.

I cannot predict if the same reverberations will befall Curtis Hanson's *8 Mile*, which similarly captures an underground culture and features a bad-boy crossover star at the center of the film.

But while Eminem's presence will guarantee initial interest, I believe *8 Mile* will be looked upon later as a definitive film about hip-hop culture.

There are so many things this film gets right that it's very easy to overlook the balls it drops. Characters are introduced and only sporadically used and some narrative strands are never followed up.

Just as hip-hop captures a street vitality and immediacy in its music, *8 Mile* is alive in every frame. Unfolding over a week in 1995 in Detroit, we meet Jimmy "Rabbit" Smith, Jr. (Eminem), a wiry and insecure steel worker who dreams of platinum sales with his core group of friends.

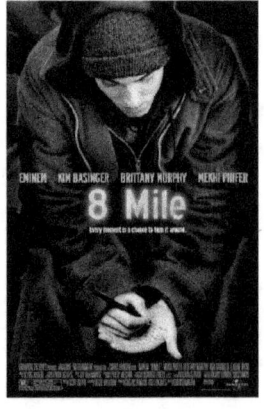

Unlike them, he is well aware of his level of poverty and lack of anything even remotely resembling a family. His living condition and place on the food chain seems to be on his mind every moment. To boot, he just broke up with his girlfriend, surrendered his car, and now has to move back in with his trailer park mom.

Jimmy enters a rap contest at a rough club and chokes on stage. That he's white certainly doesn't earn any sympathy from the black crowd. That he can't utter a single word now makes him ridiculed on the street.

Much like Rocky Balboa, Jimmy elicits immediate sympathy because he thinks - no, he *knows* without question - that he is a loser. Unlike Rocky, there is no muse or hometown support.

Kim Basinger is slightly miscast as Jimmy's trashy mom, who despite loving her son, also wouldn't know a family dinner if she woke up at one. Hanson may be the only director capable of getting a good performance from her.

Mekhi Phifer is great as Jimmy's best friend, Future, the guy who runs the rap battles and believes absolutely in Jimmy's lyrical talent. His dreadlocked mane and energy blind us to the fact that he's really just playing a hip-hop Mickey to Eminem's Rocky.

Brittany Murphy is Jimmy's skanky muse, but her character is wasted. Aside from a semi-hot sex scene and being the one person chosen to deliver all the obligatory "I got a special feeling about you" lines, Murphy's presence in this film is a confusing one. In the end, one wonders how much she really assists things, aside from just buzzing around them a lot.

Then there's Eminem (aka Marshall Mathers), the cultural lightning rod of the decade. It's no mystery that screenwriter Scott Silver drew heavily upon Em's world from back in the day, but I don't think anybody would confuse this with "The Eminem Story."

His lyrics have portrayed tormented and twisted characters, the kind that earn him magazine covers and organized protests. But even a casual listen to the full context of even his most notorious songs do not reveal any type of evil lurking so much as a brilliant, at times, self-mocking storyteller who happens to lean toward the dark side. Stephen King does it all the time but parents don't vilify him. Ah well. Welcome to being a celebrity in the 21st century.

As an actor, Eminem is no Lawrence Olivier. But at the center of this film, he occupies every frame with a combination of insecurity, rage and vulnerability. He's so believable as the weather-worn Rabbit that when he finally emerges as a more confident presence, it's rousing.

I think a comparison to James Dean is more apt.

8 Mile captures the essence of hip-hop, the vitality and immediacy of the rhymes, and the posturing of street soldiers who have become thugs because they have no other choice. Suppressed rage manifests into spontaneous explosions of rhyme, especially in

the club where the rap contests have come to mean more than just a ticket to the big time.

It's hard to imagine a rousing cinematic moment built around the concept of people insulting each other to a beat, but the freestyle bursts of lyrical violence are as cathartic as a climactic gunfight in an action movie.

There are a hundred ways *8 Mile* could have sold out and become as clichéd as *Purple Rain*, or God forbid, Mariah Carey's *Glitter*. It's almost as if director Curtis Hanson knew that people have seen this film before, which freed him to look at other things.

As opposed to the obligatory happy ending or the cautionary tragic ending, Hanson takes us out at a moment that happens to be the *right* ending.

But there is the lingering feeling that even after the credits roll and the lights come up, something bad may still happen to Jimmy. And that's one of many reasons why *8 Mile* deserves a place alongside *Saturday Night Fever*.

Despite its flaws, it captures lightning in a bottle and becomes the definitive movie of its moment, capturing what a vital youth culture is thinking and striving for.

Jimmy "Rabbit" Smith dreams of a better life and wouldn't scoff at the idea of platinum sales and bikini-clad women. But the one prize worth fighting for is the one thing that has eluded him until this moment: self-respect.

Not Quite Hollywood:
The Wild, Untold Story Of Ozploitation!

July 31, 2009

Some great films ushered forth the Australian film movement of the 1970s. Classy, elegant, acclaimed works ... that have no place in this documentary!

Instead, director Mark Hartley rips the lid off the *other* Australian cinematic explosion, the one that was a result of the abolishing of a very strict censorship code and the introduction of an R-rating (18 and over).

Overnight, cheap exploitation flicks were everywhere, filled with gratuitous sex (referred to here as "boobs, pubes and tubes"),

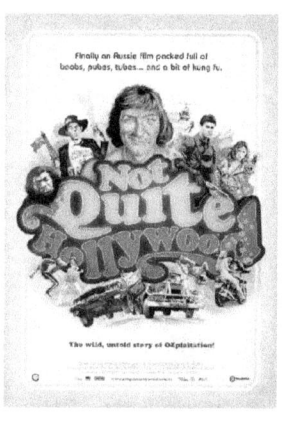

violence, gore and legitimately dangerous stunt work. *Not Quite Hollywood* is immensely entertaining, titillating and lowbrow, but also revealing a rather important lesson about artistic expression.

All pretensions aside, it's mind-boggling to watch raw footage of a drug-and-rum addled Dennis Hopper making *Mad Dog Morgan* (1976) or to hear Quentin Tarantino discuss the merits of *Patrick* (1978), a shocker about a comatose man with psychic powers; or to watch footage from *Howling III* (1987), the most bizarre werewolf movie ever conceived, right down to it's wolf-baby birth scene.

Jiggle queens Nina Landis and Candy Raymond sheepishly defend their "roles," which called for little more than being naked;

filmmakers such as John Seale talk about shooting these films as if they were conquering heroes.

Featuring interviews with over 80 directors, screenwriters and producers, including Tarantino, Brian Trenchard-Smith, Jamie Lee Curtis, Hopper (who seems embarrassed by his Mad Dog antics), George Lazenby, George Miller, Barry Humphries and Stacy Keach.

For good measure and to great effect, a couple of film critics are included to pooh-pooh all the smut.

Whether for academia's sake or just being able to find a movie that's nothing but the really good parts of other movies, *Not Quite Hollywood* is a must see!

NOTE:

The filmmakers followed *Not Quite Hollywood* with the equally-entertaining *Machete Maidens Unleashed*, which closes the loop on the idea that the low-budget wave of the early 70s actually elevated B-movie ideas to the mainstream, an idea I've heard before. *Star Wars* and *Jaws* changed summer movie-going forever, but would monster movies and haunted house flicks exist at the multiplex if not for these scrappy exploitation flicks? Discuss.

Machete Maidens Unleashed!

July 26, 2011

Mark Hartley's follow-up to *Not Quite Hollywood: The Wild, Untold Story of Ozploitation!* (2008) is another vastly entertaining doc about low-budget filmmaking and exploitation flicks, this one shining the light on the Filipino movie scene in the early 70s.

With the blessing of dictator Ferdinand Marcos, American filmmakers were able to shoot in the Philippines for next to nothing, which offered directors a chance to make more exotic movies with bigger scopes – sometimes with the Filipino army providing the stunts! The result is a glorious montage of gratuitous boobs and ridiculous action from women-in-prison flicks, revenge movies and revolution films.

Cult movie icons Roger Corman, Jack Hill, Joe Dante, John Landis, Sid Haig and Eddie Romero take turns with jaw-dropping tales about dangerous no-budget filmmaking, and offer illuminating commentary.

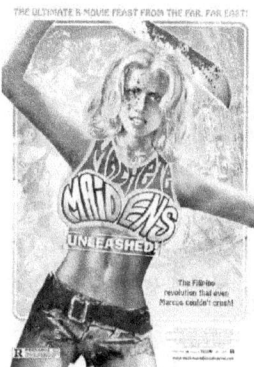

Corman, long considered the ultimate low-budget success story, is respectful and reflective enough to make you wonder whether he realized he was making junk. But the guy was no dope. He understood the logistics of the process and knew how to sell a picture, even if that meant propping up a crappy trailer with a stock shot of an exploding helicopter.

Eventually, the narrative makes an argument for exploitation movies becoming so influential that is allowed Steven Spielberg to create *Jaws* (1975), thereby elevating B-movies to the A-list status.

The section about the "women in chains" movies begs the question about the bourgeoning feminist movement of the 70s. Were women truly liberated by baring their breasts in grindhouse flicks?

Director Jon Landis, more animated than usual, steals the movie with his refreshing honesty. "I don't buy into that feminist stuff. They'll take control, but they'll show you their tits!"

Warrior

September 9, 2011

Is there any more tried and true formula for a winning drama than the boxing genre?

From *The Champ* to the ubiquitous *Rocky* films, to arty Oscar fare like Martin Scorsese's *Raging Bull* and David O. Russell's *The Fighter*, boxing flicks are a sure thing, so long as the movie gets one thing right: make the audience care enough, so that when our pugilist hero digs down and summons enough blind force to beat the snot out of his opponent, it's a sublime, soul-warming catharsis.

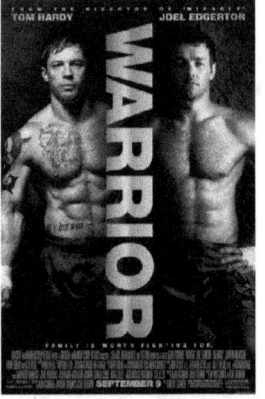

Because the fight, you see, is always the metaphor. It's never *really* about beating the other guy so much as it's about going the distance, winning the girl, proving your love or whatever the emotional conflict of the film happens to be. And yes, great boxing movies will make a grown man cry like a little girl who had her kitten taken away.

Meet the present-day fractured Conlan family: Dad Paddy (Nick Nolte) used to be a raging drunk, which is why his wife left with his sons ages ago. Years after mom's death, Tommy (Tom Hardy) is an Iraq war vet with a checkered past. He shows up on Paddy's doorstep – the old man is now one thousand days sober – but refuses to cut his sorry pop any slack.

His brother Brendan (Joel Edgerton) is now a physics teacher with a solid family but broken finances. He resents his brother and has equal disdain for their father.

But here's the thing: both brothers are fighters, in particular, mixed martial artists. Tommy has nothing to lose (he's on the run), and Brendan has everything to lose (his daughter's medical bills have threatened their home with foreclosure).

Screenwriting 101 suggests that we'll grow to root for each brother, and thanks to the revealing promos, we know that eventually, they will take all that pent up family agita into the cage with them.

What's most savvy is how the movie dodges and weaves, and delivers surprising knockouts blows when you don't expect them, even when serving up a boxing movie that never deviates from the formula. That's a compliment, mostly due to the strong performances, but also because co-writer/director Gavin O'Connor avoids the obvious as much as he can.

Hardy, who was amazing in *Bronson* (2009) and stole his scenes in *Inception* (2010), is a force of nature. Chin tucked, and ready for action at all times, he prowls the movie like a coiled animal. In any other movie, his casual cruelty would make him the villain, but a more complex picture emerges later.

Edgerton has similarly been great in movies that never hit the mainstream (*Animal Kingdom*, *The Square*) and also makes the most of his role: he initially plays Brendan as a reluctant fighter, but as the movie progresses, he reveals shades of the anger that fuel him.

Nolte has never been better, as the now-sober dad who wears every bad decision he's ever made like an uncomfortable jacket. There is also something achingly sad about an old man choosing to do penance through his sons' harsh criticisms and insults because that's the only way he can be in the same room with them.

Jennifer Morrison is Edgerton's tough, devoted wife, an Adrian for the 21st century. If you've ever seen a *Rocky* movie, you know she's the character who advises him to stay out of the ring, but won't be able to stay away from the arena.

There is a modern-day version of the "Yo Adrian, I did it!" moment (don't worry, that's not a spoiler) and it has the same rousing effect. Oh, and about that jaw-dropping finale? I'll say only this: men, bring your hankies. This flick, on its way to setting up the brother vs. brother smackdown nobody wants to see, nicely positions a handful of emotional time bombs.

Maybe it's the father-son conflicts, maybe it's the regret that fathers feel when considering their actions. Either way, *Warrior* becomes is the movie most likely to make grown men blubber since Kevin Costner asked his dad if he wanted to have a catch. It may be clichéd to the hills, but it's also brutally violent, cinematic, smart and filled with emotionally-resonant and satisfying movie moments.

aBOUT THe auTHOr

Dennis Willis is an award-winning producer, TV host, producer, director, editor, screenwriter and film critic. He produced and co-hosted the TV program *Reel Life* (later called *FilmTrip*) from 1993-98.

Mr. Willis hosts the *Flick Nation* radio show, a weekly 1-hour look at the entertainment industry from the inside out. He also hosts the weekly syndicated feature *Flick Nation: Home Media Guide,* and is the Afternoon News film critic on KGO Radio in San Francisco.

His written reviews have appeared in dozens of magazines and newspapers; and he has conducted hundreds of interviews with filmmakers and movie stars. Since 2009, Mr. Willis has published the *Flick Nation Movie Guide*, a compendium of current reviews.

denniswillis.net
flicknation.net
facebook.com/denniswillis
twitter.com/denniswillis

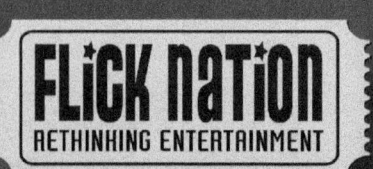
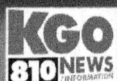 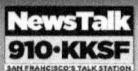 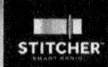
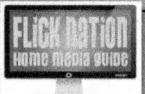

www.ingramcontent.com/pod-product-compliance
Lightning Source LLC
Chambersburg PA
CBHW051458170526
45166CB00001B/291